THROUGH THE VALLEY OF THE SHADOW

Studies in Chinese Christianity

G. Wright Doyle and Carol Lee Hamrin
Series Editors

A Project of the Global China Center
www.globalchinacenter.org

Through the Valley of the Shadow

Australian Women in War-Torn China

LINDA AND ROBERT BANKS

◆PICKWICK *Publications* • Eugene, Oregon

THROUGH THE VALLEY OF THE SHADOW
Australian Women in War-Torn China
Studies in Chinese Christianity

Copyright © 2019 Linda Banks and Robert Banks. All rights reserved. Except for brief quotations in critical publications or reviews, no part of this book may be reproduced in any manner without prior written permission from the publisher. Write: Permissions, Wipf and Stock Publishers, 199 W. 8th Ave., Suite 3, Eugene, OR 97401.

Pickwick Publications
An Imprint of Wipf and Stock Publishers
199 W. 8th Ave., Suite 3
Eugene, OR 97401

www.wipfandstock.com

PAPERBACK ISBN: 978-1-5326-8671-9
HARDCOVER ISBN: 978-1-5326-8672-6
EBOOK ISBN: 978-1-5326-8673-3

Cataloging-in-Publication data:

Names: Banks, Linda, author. | Banks, Robert, author.
Title: Through the valley of the shadow : Australian women in war-torn China / Linda Banks and Robert Banks.
Description: Eugene, OR: Pickwick Publications, 2019. | Studies in Chinese Christianity. | Includes bibliographical references.
Identifiers: ISBN: 978-1-5326-8671-9 (PAPERBACK). | ISBN: 978-1-5326-8672-6 (HARDCOVER). | ISBN: 978-1-5326-8673-3 (EBOOK).
Subjects: LCSH: Christianity—China—History—20th century. | Church history—20th century. | Missionaries—Biography.
Classification: BR1288 B36 2019 (print). | BR1288 (epub).

Manufactured in the U.S.A.

Scripture marked (KJV) is taken from the King James Version of the Bible, in the public domain.

Scripture quotations marked (NIV) are taken from the Holy Bible, NEW INTERNATIONAL VERSION®, NIV® Copyright © 1973, 1978, 1984, 2011 by Biblica, Inc.® Used by permission. All rights reserved worldwide.

To the generations of
Chinese Christians
who suffered during periods of armed conflict
in their own land

Contents

Sources of Images | ix
List of Images | xi
References to Places | xiii
Acknowledgments | xv
Prologue | xix

1 Eleanor and Elizabeth Saunders | 1
2 Victoria Mannett | 23
3 Martha and Eliza Clark | 45
4 Rhoda Watkins | 68
5 Nora Dillon | 92
   Epilogue | 116

   Bibliography | 121

Sources of Images

We are grateful for the use of the following images, courtesy:

Admiralty Official Collection, Imperial War Museum, London—34

Banks Family Collection—37

Church Missionary Society, United Kingdom—14, 18, 29, 32

Church Missionary Society, Australia—9, 16, 31

Historical Photographs of China, University of Bristol at www.hpcbristol.net—19

Howard K. Mowll Collection, State Library of Victoria—13

Jolly Family Collection—25

Mary Andrews Collection, Moore Theological College—35, 36

Mary Jane Steer and Historical Photographs of China, University of Bristol—12

Matai Shen from "Memories of Guilin"—24, 26, 27, 28

Melbourne Anglican Diocesan Archives—15, 22

Nora Dillon Collection, Moore Theological College—30

School of Oriental and African Studies, University of London—3, 6, 7, 8

Watkins Family Collection—23

The remaining images—1, 2, 4, 11, 17, 20, 21, and 33—are in the public domain.

List of Images

01　Historic Mission Map of China | xvii
02　Eleanor and Elizabeth Saunders | 1
03　CMS Mission Station at Kucheng | 6
04　The sisters in Chinese dress | 8
05　Mission Houses at Huasang | 11
06　The Mission Houses after the Attack | 19
07　Captured *Ch-ih-t-sai Ti* Leaders | 20
08　Graves in International Cemetery, Foochow | 22
09　Victoria Mannett | 23
10　Victoria with other missionaries in Mienchow 1916 | 29
11　Chinese Bandits in Western China | 33
12　Administration Building, West China Union University | 36
13　Women Education students at the University | 37
14　The Student Hostel across from the Bishop's House | 39
15　Victoria with Mary returning to Australia | 43
16　Martha and Eliza Clark | 45
17　"Bridge of Boats", Ningpo | 49
18　Trinity College in the CMS compound | 51
19　Refugees streaming into the International Settlement, Shanghai | 56
20　Japanese soldiers occupying Ningpo | 59
21　Columbia Country Club, Shanghai | 62

List of Images

22 Martha and Eliza on deputation in Australia | 66
23 Rhoda Watkins | 68
24 View over picturesque Kweilin | 73
25 Rhoda and staff with new-born babies | 77
26 Main entrance to the Way of Life Hospital | 78
27 Kweilin devastated by air raids and fire | 84
28 Remains of the hospital on Rhoda's return | 85
29 Thanksgiving for rebuilding | 87
30 Nora Dillon | 92
31 Chinese village children | 97
32 Taipo Orphanage, Hong Kong | 101
33 Japanese soldiers crossing bridge near Taipo | 103
34 British Admiral, Nora and students during Victory celebrations | 107
35 Nora, with Mary Andrews on their veranda in Shaohsing | 109
36 Shaohsing congregation shortly before Nora returned home | 112

References to Places

TO PRESERVE HISTORICAL ACCURACY, earlier place-names have been retained in the text. The following list shows their modern equivalents.

Canton (Guangzhou)
Chekiang (Zhejiang)
Chengtu (Chengdu)
Chungking (Chonqing)
Foochow (Fuzhou)
Formosa (Taiwan)
Fukien (Fujian)
Hangchow (Hangzhou)
Hangkow (Hankou)
Kiangsi (Jiangsu)
Kucheng (Gutian)
Kwangsi (Guangxi)
Kwantung (Guangzhong)
Limchow (Lianzhou)
Mienchow (Mianyang)
Nanking (Nanjing)
Ningpo (Ningbo)
Peking (Beijing)
Shantung (Shandong)
Shaohsing (Shaoxing)
Szechwan (Sichuan)

Earlier distance measurements have also been retained: references are therefore to feet rather than centimeters, and to miles rather than kilometers.

Acknowledgments

THE CREATION OF A book is a process involving the help of many people and institutions. We are deeply indebted to the following for their contribution towards this volume.

For family and personal records:
  Betty Blackmore
  Kath Collett
  Elaine & Lurline Dillon-Smith
  Ken & Jan Goodlet
  Bill & Ros Hague
  David & Ann Hewetson
  Marilyn & David Jolly
  Ted & Morwen Watkins

For research materials:
  Dr. Patricia P. K. Chiu, Hong Kong University
  Prof. Chen Jianming, Professor Sichuan University, Chengdu
  Dr. Liao Robert, Women and Children's Hospital, Guilin
  Lyn Milton, Chief Archivist, CMS Australia, Sydney
  Prof. Peter Ng, Adjunct Professor, Shanghai University
  Matai Shen, Guilin
  Prof. Philip Wickeri, Ming Hwa Theological College, Hong Kong
  Bai Xiaoyun, Mianyang Teacher's College, Sichuan

Acknowledgments

Anglican Diocese Archives, Melbourne
Hong Kong Baptist University
Melbourne School of Theology
Moore Theological College, Sydney
National Library of Australia, Canberra
Ridley College, Melbourne
St Mark's Library, Canberra
State Library of Victoria, Melbourne
Sydney Missionary and Bible College
Trinity Theological College, Singapore

For Chinese Translation:
George Ngu, Edmonton, Canada
Dr. Xiaxia Xue, China Graduate School of Theology, Hong Kong
Yun Zhou, Australian National University China Institute, Canberra

For Overseas Accommodation:
Nelson & Davina Yuen, Hong Kong
Anglican Mission House, Singapore

For Financial Assistance:
E. K. Cole Publishing Fund, CMS Victoria, Melbourne
Andrew & Irene Lu, Sydney

Historic Mission Map of China

Prologue

OVER THE SIX DECADES between Hudson Taylor's visit to Australia and the Communist victory in China, missionaries began to go from one of the newest nations in the world to one of the oldest. In 1890 Australia was just a century old, still drawing immigrants from overseas. Now, hearing about desperate needs in China, some of its people began volunteering to go there. Among those who went, eighty percent were women. These were mostly young, single, with varying degrees of education, who came from several Australian states. The five stories that follow focus on the lives of women, all members of the Church Missionary Society,[1] who served in China during periods of armed conflict. All, except two, who died young, worked there most of their adult lives. All displayed remarkable resilience and left a lasting legacy in their adopted country.[2]

In China, armed conflict was nothing new. It has been part of the fabric of that country for centuries.[3] In the period from 1890 to 1950, it took various forms.

First, occasional attacks by local or regional groups who violently opposed the current regime and foreign influence. These culminated in the Boxer Uprising in northern China from 1899 to 1900. Though based among the peasantry,

---

1. On the work of this Anglican organization in various countries during this period see Cole, *Church Missionary Society*, especially 139–52 on China. The main other organization which sent Australian missionaries to China was the China Inland Mission, whose work is described in Brotchie, "China Inland Mission". On Australian women missionaries in China more generally in this period see Dixon, Australian Missionary Endeavour. The role of women in this Mission is discussed by Griffiths, *Not Less Than Everything*, which covers from the mid 1800s to the late 1900s.

2. The major work on the development of Christianity in China during these decades as well as more widely is Bays, *A New History*, 82–121.

3. So Durschmied, *Military History of China*, particularly 156–222 for the period this book examines.

Prologue

these groups were sometimes backed by local authorities and government officials.

Second, raids by bandits in the countryside during the declining decades of the Qing dynasty. These were often in response to the poverty created by natural disasters, especially famine. Over the years the ranks of such groups were often swelled by deserters from regional armies that had suffered defeat.

Third, the rise of local and provincial warlords alongside the central government's weakening forces, especially in outlying provinces. These generals continually fought each other for supremacy in various cities and regions. On occasions they also fought for independence against whoever was in power in the central government.

Fourth, the struggle to defeat the Imperial dynasty and replace it with a Republican constitution. This culminated in the success of the Nationalist Revolution in 1911 and, after its short-lived victory, the campaign to restore the Republic in the mid-1920s. In the intervening period, conflicts between warlords and central authorities largely dominated China.

Fifth, the formation of the Communist movement in the 1920s and its gradual increase in influence. After its purge by the Nationalists in 1927, hostilities escalated between the two. Apart from their temporary alliance during the second Sino-Japanese War, military rivalry resurfaced until the Communist triumph in 1949.

Sixth, intermittent warfare between Japan and China throughout this whole period. This began with Japan's attacks on Korea, a Chinese protectorate, and on Formosa in the mid-1890s. In 1933 Japan then occupied Manchuria. This led to its full invasion of China in 1937 that became part of the Second World War.

Seventh, large scale student-led demonstrations in several Chinese cities. These began in 1895 as a consequence of Japan's attack on Korea. In 1919, when the Treaty of Versailles gave Japan greater influence in Shantung province, a series of organized anti-Western, increasingly anti-Christian, demonstrations took place. Though these were mainly non-violent, occasionally they resulted in loss of life.[4]

The scale and impact of these conflicts in China is much less well known than the wars that ravaged Europe during the same period. According to some historians, however, their cumulative effect on the people and nation actually exceeds the ruin and destruction caused by both the two World Wars and Russian Revolution.

---

4. The work that best documents the kinds of armed conflict in China throughout this period is Zarrow, *War in China, 1895–1950*.

Prologue

The women in this volume were all caught up in, and personally affected by, one or more of these conflicts. This was not just because they were foreigners but because they identified with the local community and its people, frequently suffering with them and taking risky actions to protect them. Living in war-zones had a deep impact on their experience of God, relationships with fellow-christians, attitude to their enemies, and views of the future. Drawing on their diaries, personal correspondence, official annual letters, missionary publications and archives, newspaper articles, family reminiscences and biographical resources, we have sought to bring their stories to life for our generation, not only in Australia and China but in Asia and the West more generally.[5]

Much of this material, however, only allows us partial entry into their innermost thoughts and feelings. Annual letters to their Mission's headquarters largely contained reports of their work that mostly excluded deeply personal reactions. Missionary publications frequently censored what were perceived as negative stories, and during times of extreme conflict communication from the field was limited and often out of date. Their personal letters home, when they got through, did not always reveal the whole story for fear of creating anxiety among family and friends.

Recording these women's largely unknown stories is a way of honoring and, most of all, learning from them. They deserve more, but certainly no less.

---

5. The multifaceted relationship between Australia and China is helpfully explored in Walker, *Anxious Nation,* 2nd. ed.

1

Eleanor and Elizabeth Saunders

荀內莉—荀姑娘
Pastoral Workers—Kucheng

Eleanor and Elizabeth Saunders

SHORTLY BEFORE THEIR SHIP was due to depart, Eleanor and Elizabeth Saunders, together with their mother Eliza, arrived in Sydney. They had travelled over five hundred miles from their home in Melbourne by overnight express train. After arranging for their trunks and luggage to be conveyed to the Millers Point dock, they planned to meet the local committee of the

Church Missionary Association (CMA).[1] Though they had already been officially fare-welled in Melbourne, people in Sydney were eager to meet the first missionaries their organization had sent to China, one of whom was the youngest it had ever accepted.

The *SS Menmuir* was a small passenger cargo ship that made regular trips between Australia and Asia. This one-stack, two-masted steamer, loaded with thirteen hundred tons of coal and some international mail, was bound for Hong Kong via Brisbane, Cooktown, Darwin and Manila.[2] Along with Eleanor and Elizabeth Saunders, on board were three other missionaries, a Chinese couple returning to Shanghai, a single woman and several soldiers. Mrs. Saunders was accompanying her daughters until Brisbane.

On 13 October 1893, just before the ship's departure, a group gathered for a brief informal service on deck. Present that Saturday afternoon were representatives of several denominations, two mission societies, a few young women interested in becoming missionaries, and some local Chinese Christians.[3] After singing the final hymn, the visitors left and the ship made its way past Garden Island, through Sydney Heads and out to sea.

Two days later the ship docked in Brisbane, where the Saunders sisters said final goodbyes to their mother. Knowing how difficult this moment would be, they had made a pact to shed no tears when the time came. Despite this, as the lights on the wharf faded into the distance, Elizabeth, the younger of the two, cradled her head on the ship's railing and sobbed.

At daybreak, passing through the Great Barrier Reef, the two young women were wretchedly seasick. After leaving Cooktown, a day later, they were invited to join the captain and officers for breakfast. As Eleanor wrote in her first letter home: "We are getting close to Port Darwin now. This morning we passed an island 150 miles long: it is all cannibals. Captain said at breakfast that it was a good field for missionaries—sarcastically, of course—and we asked him to put us down, but he said he had too much respect for us!"[4]

Feeling better, they now enjoyed spending time on deck, observing the passing islands and vibrant sunsets, trying to make conversation with the

---

1. At this time only Melbourne and Sydney had Church Missionary Associations. These had recently become semi-autonomous auxiliaries, rather than just branches, of the Church Missionary Society in the United Kingdom.

2. A photo of the ship in Sydney Harbor can be accessed at https://collection.maas.museum/object/31755.

3. Among those were two future missionaries, Sophie Newton and Amy Oxley, whose biographies we have written. See our books *Faraway Pagoda* and *See His Face*.

4. Their letters are reproduced in Berry, *Sister Martyrs*, 10. This book contains the most extensive collection of personal letters from the two sisters, but see also the more abridged selection later provided in Cole, *Letters From China*.

Chinese lady, and writing home. Eleanor's correspondence displayed an eye for descriptive, at times witty, detail. Elizabeth's letters, which had occasional humorous touches, were more reflective and emotionally charged. As she confessed: "If I can't write just as I feel inclined to, then nothing will go out at all."[5]

Because they had much in common with the other three new missionaries, getting to know them did not take long. Though these women were several years older than the two sisters, all were soon on familiar terms. Eleanor and Elizabeth introduced themselves by their nicknames, Nellie and Topsy. The others were Ellie McCulloch, Ethel Reid and Harriet Fleming.

Most evenings they took turns to invite each other for supper in their cabins. On these occasions the women opened up about what they were doing before leaving for China. Nellie was training to become a professional pianist and Topsy preparing to be a private tutor. To their surprise, all found they had first become interested in the needs of women and children in China through hearing Hudson Taylor when he visited Melbourne in 1889.[6] At the time Nellie and Topsy were only in their teens, and it wasn't until the visit three years later by Rev Robert Stewart, a CMS missionary in Fukien Province, that they were able to respond to God's call to go. Despite only being young—Nellie was only twenty-two and Topsy just twenty—after some theological and medical training the CMA was willing to send them if chaperoned by their widowed mother. All this depended on Mrs. Saunders selling the family home to fund her support. However, the widespread 1890s Depression prevented this plan eventuating. Only when Robert and his wife Louisa Stewart guaranteed they would look after the girls in Kucheng, did the CMA agree to let them go.[7]

One evening after a Bible study with the other women, Topsy asked whether they ever felt afraid about going to China. Recalling Robert Stewart's story of two female missionaries who were beaten, dragged through the crowd and, for a time, hung upside-down at the town gate, Topsy had often wondered how she would respond in similar circumstances.[8] One of the women said that while members of her China Inland Mission (CIM) had occasionally encountered a hostile reception, especially from men, this had rarely led to any physical threat. Only a handful of its more than a thousand missionaries had been killed. Though tensions were increasing between some elements of Chinese society and foreigners, so far these were intermittent.

---

5. Berry, *Sister Martyrs*, 103.

6. An account of his visit may be found in Dr. and Mrs. Taylor, *Hudson*, 488–96.

7. Further background on the two sisters can be found in Welch, "Nellie, Topsy and Annie."

8. *Goulburn Evening Penny Post*, 22 September 1892, 4.

One evening Nellie arranged for the small organ she was bringing from Australia to be carried up from the hold. As the group sang hymns in the cabin, one of the officers joined them and several soldiers hung around outside to listen. Although no church services were scheduled for Sundays, several of the crew suggested the women organize one. Accustomed to only clergyman speaking on such occasions, they wanted to hear what young women had to say. At the first service, Topsy and Ethel spoke, while Nellie accompanied the singing. As word about this spread around the ship, it opened up conversation with a number of people about Christianity.

The two sisters became firm friends with the second and third mates as well as the purser. These men were initially surprised to find that the two young, tall and attractive women did not fit their stereotype of a missionary. Both were full of fun, who enjoyed playing games and outdoor activities.[9] The following Sunday, as the ship neared Manila, though no mention had been made of a service being held, "at breakfast all three appeared, got dressed up to kill, with lovely white shirts and their dark blue coats, with the gold braid and buttons on."[10]

While the ship unloaded its cargo in Manila, Nellie and Topsy had time to visit historic and poorer parts of the city and take a scenic trip up-river to the lake at Laguna de Bay. After leaving port, they enjoyed relaxing some evenings with senior members of the crew. As Nellie writes: "They all demanded the baby organ and hymns. It is really almost touching to see those great big things that spend most of their time playing poker and drinking when we are not about, listening to the hymns, and they do like them so . . . they are also eager to talk. We never have to make an opportunity of speaking [about God], because they rarely want to speak about anything else."[11]

Crossing the South China Sea to Hong Kong was very rough. As Nellie writes: "About 11, I was dragged out on to the lower deck and planted in a chair where I remained till it capsized and nearly smashed me to atoms. Then I went inside and lay on the bathroom floor, an utter wreck, until after dinner."[12] They arrived at their destination "nearly dead." Added to this, feelings of sadness swept over them as they said goodbye to the captain and senior officers. The captain, who was normally quite reserved, reminded them of the evening

---

9. In the *Church Missionary Intelligencer*, September 1895, 140, their first Vicar, Rev S. Mercer, described the girls at a younger age as typically Australian: "happy . . . buoyant . . . full of life, somewhat wayward and difficult to control . . . much in request for music, dancing and lawn-tennis."

10. See Berry, *Sister Martyrs*, 13.

11. Berry, *Sister Martyrs*, 14.

12. Berry, *Sister Martyrs*, 23.

they fare-welled their mother on board. When promising to keep an eye on her daughters, he was deeply moved by hearing Nellie whisper to her mother: "We have Someone better!"[13] The second and third mates also promised to visit Mrs. Saunders whenever the ship was in Melbourne and that the next time it berthed in Foochow they would pass on parcels and gifts from home.

經過死蔭的幽谷

During their brief transit in Hong Kong, Nellie and Topsy were too weary to see anything of the British colony. They briefly met some members of the English CMS who afterwards commented on their degree of independence but put this down to their being Australians! Transferring to a smaller boat, the *Haitian*, they began the three-day journey to Fukien Province. On board with them were the Stewart's nurse, Lena Yallop, and children, who were to be joined by Robert and Louisa when the boat reached Foochow. As it passed the island known as Sharp Peak and began sailing up the Min River, the boat was surrounded by mountains dotted with little villages and terraced rice fields. At last the sisters could see people and their homes, and had to pinch themselves that they were actually in China.

The Bund in Foochow was modest in comparison with the imposing one in Shanghai but a sizeable crowd was there to greet them. They were taken to the home of Archdeacon John Wolfe and his Australian wife Mary. She greeted them by their Chinese names: Nellie's was Sung Ku-niong Nali and Topsy's Sung Ne Ku-niong Tosi. ("Ku-niong" meant dedicated woman and "Ne" second). A week later they were delighted to meet up with Robert and Louisa Stewart who were arriving back in the province after an extended leave. The couple showed them around the major sites in the Old City—the imposing White and Black Pagodas, the ancient Bridge of Ten Thousand Ages, and the beautiful Palace Gardens.

Alongside these impressive sites, they also saw many orphan children, especially girls, women with bound and misshapen feet and, in the distance by the river, the so-called "baby-towers" where unwanted girls were discarded and washed away. Passing Trinity College, which Robert Stewart had founded, they were told how several years before a violent student demonstration had resulted in its being set alight, several people injured, and the Stewarts fleeing for their lives.[14]

---

13. Berry, *Sister Martyrs*, 6.

14. The early history of Christian work in Fukien province was written by Eugene Stock, who the Saunders sisters had met in Melbourne: see his *Christ and Fukien*, 10–22.

Finally, on 13 December 1893, their party set out for the remote city of Kucheng, ninety miles inland. This involved travelling two days by hired houseboats and their crews, and one day by foot and sedan chair. Soon Nellie and Topsy found themselves surrounded by towering mountains that were shrouded in mist. The hillsides were dotted with decorative Buddhist temples, one of which they stepped ashore to visit. Their hearts ached when they saw worshippers prostrating themselves before statues of idols.

The second evening the group disembarked at the small river port of Sui Kau. The following day they ascended a narrow path with their loads of baggage hauled by Chinese porters. At times, when the path was particularly steep, they were carried in sedan chairs, with occasional stops while porters had an opium break. By mid-afternoon they were met by a welcoming group of Chinese Christians from Kucheng who escorted them to the mission station. They arrived just after six in the evening.

Kucheng was the first center outside Foochow where the CMS Mission had established a base. There was also an American missionary presence in the area. This district capital had a population of around fifty thousand and was surrounded by numerous villages. The two sisters were immediately struck by the press of people, high level of noise, crowded narrow lanes, carts drawn by animals, vibrant red and gold characters on buildings, laundry poles hanging out windows, blind and disabled beggars on the streets, and smells—both fragrant and unsanitary.

CMS Mission Station at Kucheng

The mission station, situated on a steep hill outside the city wall, comprised four dwellings. There was the Stewart's two-storey house, where initially Nellie and Topsy were to stay. Nearby were two large bungalows for missionaries on break from their outlying centers—Elsie Marshall, Hessie Newcombe, Flora Codrington and Flora Stewart, (no relation)—all from Great Britain. "The Bird's Nest" baby orphanage, where two Australians Ada Nisbet and Annie Gordon worked, was also within the compound.[15]

The sisters were especially looking forward to catching up with Annie Gordon. Though hailing from Queensland, they had met her while she was doing her missionary training in Melbourne. The orphanage itself was well known in the Saunders's household because they had prayed regularly for Ada Nisbet, who came from Tasmania, and the children. It was wonderful to hear an Australian accent again. Over the next couple of weeks, the two women gave Nellie and Topsy a helpful orientation to living in the district.

It was very clear that the Stewarts worked as a partnership. Robert oversaw its wide range of ministries and Louisa supervised educational work in the region. Since most of the missionaries in Kucheng were younger women, she took responsibility for their welfare. Louisa was also the most gifted Chinese speaker and, according to Nellie, one of the "sweetest" women she had ever met. The girls soon began to feel at home. Nellie wrote to her mother: "Mr Stewart is a dear . . . He parades around the place in a huge pith helmet, and after meals you hear the melodious sound of his cornet, playing hymn tunes, and occasionally he and Mrs Stewart have concerts," adding humorously "When I came into the drawing room . . . I told them the police were coming!"[16]

On another occasion, Nellie described how they had learnt to eat some unusual Chinese dishes. Mr Stewart's strategy for eating slugs was "put them into your mouth, swallow them as quickly as possible, and say Amen."[17] The sisters did not take long to adjust to a very different diet but they still appreciated receiving occasional food parcels from home, especially on their first Christmas. In order to identify with the local people, all the missionaries wore Chinese clothing. Initially Nellie and Topsy bought a red skirt typically worn by local women, a blue coat for everyday wear, umbrella, and a Manchu style outfit for more formal occasions.

---

15. These two women served with the Church of England Zenana Missionary Society, a precursor to CMS in Australia.

16. Berry, *Sister Martyrs*, 38–39.

17. Berry, *Sister Martyrs*, 12.

The sisters in Chinese dress

The girls' first responsibility was to learn the local dialect. This was different to both Mandarin and Cantonese, and even what was spoken in Foochow. They were each allocated a Chinese teacher with whom they studied four to five hours a day. Nellie, the more natural linguist, obtained basic proficiency in just six months, half the usual time. It took Topsy longer to pass the exams because she found it easier to learn the language through conversation with local people. In general, Nellie was the more confident and outgoing, while her sister was more retiring and preferred working one to one. Always the less physically robust of the two, Topsy was more prone to tropical diseases and emotional highs and lows. Partly for this reason she was keen to add to her medical skills and spent time learning these from Dr Gregory in the nearby American Methodist Mission Hospital.

In early February 1894, during Chinese New Year, they took part in an annual conference for local Christians. The majority of attenders were women, reflecting the Mission's strategy of women reaching women and, through them, their families. Although the Kucheng Mission was based near the city, its main work was carried on in large villages one or two days walk away that could only be visited by mountain paths. This was where the women were based most of the time. Each centre ran three-month long classes for women, day schools for boys and girls, a small clinic and church. The missionaries regularly made short visits to smaller villages to care for those in need and share their faith. Such trips often involved bringing along food and sometimes even their beds!

Within a few months the sisters were attempting to teach in Chinese. Nellie was located with Annie Gordon at Dong-gio, while Topsy was placed with Elsie Marshall at Sek Chek Du. Each of these centers had responsibility for a mountainous area of a few hundred square miles. As Robert Stewart later recounted:

> Miss Nellie has daily two classes of charming boys, aged from twelve to sixteen, picked out from the whole District . . . They will be teachers in five or ten years hence. She also has a fine lot of women on Sunday mornings, and a Day School on Saturday afternoons, and village visiting every week. Miss Topsy . . . has Women's classes, Girl's and Boy's schools, a little dispensary, and any amount of visiting—people coming to her and she going to them.[18]

While many Westerners in China tended to treat their porters like servants, Nellie and Topsy took time to get to know them. Their friendliness gradually won over these hard-bitten men who came to regard them warmly. Initially on these trips, the sisters found villagers rather intimidating. Sometimes they would crowd around them and shout so loud that it was impossible to be heard. Those who had never seen a foreigner before would often come up close, stare at them, and ask directly: How old are you? Where do you come from? How many children do you have? Why is your face so white? How much did your dress cost? Where is your husband?

---

18. Letter from Robert Stewart, dated 18 June 1895, to Australian CMS representative E.A. Barnett in Hong Kong in the Sydney *Daily Telegraph*, 9 August 1895, 2.

Though occasionally men would forbid the sisters to talk to their wives, mostly Nellie and Topsy found people friendly and were offered a place to stay. As Nellie commented later: "It's just lovely going about in the country. Everyone is always so glad to see us; of course they stare and make remarks, but that can hardly be wondered at."[19] However, there were some real challenges. Accommodation was very basic—tiny lofts, back rooms, or small barns with the animals—that was open to the elements with little privacy. This made it difficult to undress, wash and go to the toilet. Now and again they confronted a more insidious challenge. Some men thought that, since unaccompanied by a husband, they were "loose women," open to sexual advances. As a protection, the ladies always travelled with a male pastoral assistant or at least a couple of porters.

Initially Nellie and Topsy were surprised at how hard it was for Chinese women to understand the gospel message. Even though this was usually given by a convert travelling with them:

> It seems so strange to these women to think there is a God who cares for them, that they can't understand it at all at first. Some of them indeed most of them are not at all happy, they have never known what it is for anyone to love them or care much about their welfare, spiritual or otherwise; and the idea that any one should care enough to want to tell them about God is quite too much for them to comprehend.[20]

In response to the poverty around them, the sisters sought to live as simply as possible. "The Chinese Christians are very poor, it is the same here as it was in the days when Jesus Himself was on earth, 'the common people heard Him gladly' . . . and you feel that there must be nothing in your house, or in your style of living, that makes them think you are very rich. The Stewarts' house is almost mean in its utter simplicity."[21]

經過死蔭的幽谷

As a policy, members of the Kucheng Mission were encouraged to take short breaks from their work during the year. It had two houses on Flower Mountain in the small village of Huasang overlooking Kucheng. This was almost fifteen hundred feet higher than the city and could be reached by sedan chair in four hours or around six by foot. The air in Huasang was cool and pure with

---

19. Berry, *Sister Martyrs*, 100.
20. Berry, *Sister Martyrs*, 59.
21. Berry, *Sister Martyrs*, 103.

views of both the city and mountains. In summer months, when the heat became unbearable on the plain and most Chinese ceased work, the missionaries relaxed together and held their annual conference. As part of this they held a small week-long series of meetings involving devotional talks, bible studies and group prayer modelled on, and held at the same time as, the large annual Keswick Convention in the Lake District in England. Most of the missionaries had been influenced by the spirituality and lifestyle encouraged by the Keswick Movement that inspired Christians in various parts of the world.[22] The time they spent at Huasang also gave them opportunity to catch up with some American missionaries from the Kucheng district who they saw only occasionally during the year.

Mission Houses at Huasang

In July 1894, Nellie was at Huasang while her sister set off for a retreat center at Sharp Peak. Topsy had heard from one of the officers on the SS *Menmuir* that it would soon be stopping at Pagoda Anchorage and that he had some packages to give them, including presents for her twenty first birthday. From Dr. Gregory's summer residence, she could see the steamers entering and leaving the expansive Min River.

22. On the development, character and influence of this Convention on the worldwide missionary movement, including in Australia, see Banks, "Keswick Movement," 49–72.

In early August both sisters heard independently that war had broken out between China and Japan over the latter's increasing intrusion in Korea that had long been a Chinese protectorate. In its quest to modernise, Japan had developed a stronger industrial base than China, for which it needed more raw materials outside its borders. As China was modernising more slowly, and had a weaker military capacity, Japan believed it could displace it from Korea and gain access to that country's store of key metals.

Its army invaded the northern province of Shandong and Manchuria, and shortly afterwards invaded Formosa, across the straits from Fukien. The loss of five thousand troops in Formosa led to Chinese forces being withdrawn from inland areas to defend the coastline.[23] Shortly after Japan invaded Korea, the prospect of war gave a passage from one of Paul's letters a deeper significance: "if we are indeed to be given that highest of all honors which Paul prayed for, to know 'the fellowship of His sufferings', it certainly cannot be by having everything just as we want it. We can but pray and . . . trust."[24]

Around this time, Robert Stewart heard rumors of a traditionalist antigovernment group occasionally gathering in the mountains around Kucheng. He was now beginning to receive first-hand reports that, because Chinese soldiers were being withdrawn from the interior of the province, this movement was gaining momentum in the district. The *Ch-ih-t-sai Ti*—referred to as "Vegetarians" by Westerners because of their food preferences—was primarily opposed to the Imperial dynasty and supporting provincial authorities because of their openness to certain foreign influence. It objected to any ideas and values that drew Chinese away from their traditional way of life, religion, and even food.[25] As such it was a precursor of the Boxer Uprising which a few years later openly challenged the Qing Dynasty and the influence of Western powers upon it.

It was not long before an incident occurred at a village not far from Kucheng. A group of *Ch-ih-t-sai Ti* pillaged shops, carried off part of a rice harvest and attacked some new converts. When local officials investigated the disturbance, they were met by an armed mob and had to withdraw. Over the next few months, Stewart was in regular contact with the chief Mandarins in Kucheng, as well as the British Consul in Foochow, about the potential threat of *Ch-ih-t sai Ti* militancy. Meanwhile the American Consul, through his network of informants, was monitoring the situation and reporting it to the US administration in Washington. Despite signs that munitions were being

---

23. More detail on this can be found throughout Paine, *Sino–Japanese War*.
24. Paul's words come from Phil 3:10; Berry, *Sister Martyrs*, 121–22.
25. On the contested make-up of this group see especially Welch, "Vegetarians," 26–29.

smuggled into the province, both Consuls underestimated the potential significance of what was happening.[26]

After the summer break, the Kucheng Mission continued work as usual. An unexpected highlight was the Mandarin's invitation to the Stewarts to bring several of their colleagues to dinner. His two wives and twenty-four daughters supervised this lavish affair that lasted long into the night. The occasion marked a new level of recognition by the local authorities of the value of missionary work in the area.[27]

It was not long, however, before signs of potential trouble began to appear. In October, Stewart became personally involved in a local incident. A legal dispute arose between some *Ch-ih-t sai Ti* and a christian man in one of the villages. They objected to him displaying the Ten Commandments on the lintels of his house and threatened him if he refused to take them down. The case went to court in Kucheng and Stewart, who had once trained as a lawyer, defended the man. This led to the arrest of four members of the movement. When other *Ch-ih-t-sai Ti* threatened the magistrate, fearful of retaliation he released the four men. Shortly afterwards, a group of three hundred members of the movement burned a Chinese christian's harvest, locked four villagers who informed Stewart about this in the chapel, and threatened to burn it down. When soldiers came to rescue the men, the *Ch-ih-t-sai Ti* overpowered them but fortunately left without setting fire to the building.[28]

In January, after celebrating a second Christmas in Kucheng, Nellie wrote home about a young married woman who had joined one of the village classes while her husband was away on business. When he returned and found one of his wives associating with missionaries, he called on the *Ch-ih-t sai Ti* to help bring her back. A small group came with the husband and forcefully took away the girl who, much to Nellie's horror, was then sold on to an opium-dealer.[29]

In early February 1895, the christians in the district gathered for their annual New Year conference in Kucheng. The build-up of *Ch-ih-t-sai Ti* activity in the region was one of the main items discussed. Stewart reported that he had informed the British Consul about this several times but had not received any serious response. He offered to write again on the Conference's behalf, stressing its members' growing anxiety at the situation. Those attending were careful, however, not to allow the local political situation to overshadow the

---

26. On the nature of diplomatic reports at this time and during the following year, see also Welch, "Murder and Diplomacy."

27. For a full description see Berry, *Sister Martyrs*, 130–34.

28. See Nellie's letter to her mother in Cole, *Letters from China*, 69–70.

29. Cole, *Letters from China*, 86.

baptism of over sixty adults who wished to publicly declare their faith. Nellie and Topsy had worked among several of these people.

Towards the end of March, the missionaries in Kucheng heard that a three thousand strong force was massing to attack the city. Its first objective was to overrun and loot the Mission houses near the city gates. Nellie considered the possibility that this "might result in one or two of us being killed, but that would not retard their plans."[30] The Mandarin warned the population that the *Ch-ih-t- sai Ti*'s intention was to displace him and take control of Kucheng. Since there was no longer a single professional soldier left in the city, on Thursday 28 March the Mandarin ordered all gates to be shut. Nellie describes what happened over the next few days:

> There was no going either in or out except by ladder which was only put down at stated times. There was a guard all around the city wall . . . On Saturday the trouble increased. The Vegetarians were still meditating a raid and were gathered in large numbers not far from Kucheng and our anxiety was not a little increased by hearing that Sek Chek Du was appointed as the rendezvous . . . A messenger was sent flying post haste to Elsie and Topsy to tell them to come in immediately. Another move to Huasang was decided on . . . but we were stopped by the sudden appearance of the Mission caretaker to tell us that the Vegetarians were planning a raid on our houses there.[31]

In response, the Mandarin posted a guard all around the city. This was made up of christians as he considered them the most trustworthy. He told the inhabitants that if they could prevent intruders coming into the city for five days, soldiers would arrive from Foochow to restore stability. This was either a bluff or a vain hope. He also insisted that the CMS missionaries come into the American mission compound in Kucheng. Those, like Nellie, who were already at the mission station outside the city were able to climb over the ladders quickly. Couriers had to be sent to others in surrounding centers telling them to return immediately. Shortly after a message came from the Consul that all missionaries should evacuate to Foochow until the disturbance was over. Stewart, however, felt it was his responsibility to stay with the local christians in Kucheng in case they were threatened.

During April there were two significant developments.[32] First, negotiations between the *Ch-ih-t- sai Ti* and the Mandarin led to a truce that avoided

---

30. On 7 April, in Cole, *Letters from China*, 100.
31. Cole, *Letters from China*, 98.
32. On this and what follows see further Welch, "Murder and Diplomacy."

armed conflict. Second, the Qing Government struck a truce with Japan that permanently ceded Formosa to it. In May, with stability formally restored to the region, the sisters and their colleagues were able to return to their centres. For the next two months the Mission continued its work until the annual summer retreat. Towards the end of June, however, Topsy talked about having to cancel visiting a village only three miles away from her mission station at Sek Chek because of heightened *Ch-ih-t sai Ti* activity. If the danger came closer, she added, "we know, and have proved . . . that God is a stronghold in the day of trouble."[33] Although reports were reaching the American Consul in Foochow that, since the truce in Kucheng, *Ch-ih-t-sai Ti* were involved in a range of criminal acts, these did not affect anyone in the Mission. Consequently, on 3 July they felt free to go to Huasang for their annual summer retreat.

經過死蔭的幽谷

In a letter written after arriving in Huasang, Louisa Stewart describes the context and setting of what happened next:

> It was really the Japanese coming south and threatening to bombard Foochow that gave the Vegetarians courage to threaten an attack on Kucheng. They are really rebels against their own Government, but they have small chance of doing any mischief except in times of trouble from an outside foe . . .
>
> The children and Lena went up about a fortnight before we did [to our summer quarters], as the heat was very great at Kucheng, and we could not leave till the work closed for the summer. Monday, Topsy Saunders came from her country station. Tuesday we packed up . . . Next day, Wednesday, we got up early to send off our loads before the sun got very hot . . . and we . . . decided to walk all the way, twelve miles. We could not start till the day began to cool, but as there was a moon it did not matter. The first part of our walk was very flat, and led along by the bed of the river, and just as it was getting dusk, we reached the foot of the mountain . . . The moon soon rose, and we had quite light enough to see our way, and it was so beautifully cool and the mountain air so fresh we did not get very tired. The last piece is a very steep pull, and we sat down to rest before attempting it. We were met there by a man with a lantern, who had come from the house to meet us. We got in about ten o'clock and found the little girls still up watching for us . . .

---

33. In Perth's *West Australian*, 24 August 1895, 5.

It has been rather wet since we came up, so we have not been able to go out much, but it is such a change from Kucheng; we can actually have a blanket on at night and enjoy it! We had a new room built on to the house this year, which is a great improvement. It makes a fine big nursery, and the former little nursery we have given to Nellie and Topsy Saunders, so we have a large family!

In the house next door we have Hessie Newcombe, Flora Codrington, Lucy Stewart; and two others are coming shortly, Elsie Marshall and Annie Gordon . . .[34] We are feeling much the better for our change to this cool place—not one ill. Is not that cause for great thankfulness to God? . . . It is such a pretty place too. We spend our days very quietly; we have to stay indoors till 5 o'clock, and we spend the time at lessons, reading aloud, writing letters, and looking after the children. From 5 o'clock to 7 o'clock all who are inclined go for a walk, and the sisters from the other house join us. Some days they go to the village and talk to the women, and twice a week come here for prayer and Bible-reading. Sunday Robert and I go to the village and have a sort of informal service . . . more come when there are not too many of us 'foreigners' together. One old man seemed really interested. He has come several times, and last Sunday he turned to the rest of the congregation and said, 'Truly the words are good. They say our sins can be forgiven, and that the Saviour died for us, and will allow us to go to His home in Heaven.' He gave them a second edition of what we had been saying. We were very glad, for it showed us he had taken it all in himself . . .

The two little boys are very well just now. Herbert is growing much stronger than he was; just at this moment they are together in a swing we had put up in the verandah. Evan sits in the middle of the seat and Herbert stands with one foot on each side of him, and works the swing up ever so high. They scream so loudly with delight that Lena has to rush out to hush them every now and then, to let baby sleep."[35]

During their Keswick-style conference in the last week of July the group met together for bible study, devotional talks, hymn singing and prayer. The final session was about Jesus' transfiguration on a mountain, revealing his divine glory to the disciples shortly before his death. They closed their time

---

34. When the remaining two arrived, Flora Codrington moved to a house a little lower down the hill owned by an American missionary Mabel Hartford.

35. The following quote combines extracts from the last two letters written by Louisa Stewart from Huasang on 6 and 19 July, which were only received later in August. See Watson, *Robert and Louisa Stewart*, 139–140.

together by saying a prayer of dedication to "present ourselves, our souls and bodies, to be a reasonable and holy and living sacrifice to God" (paraphrase of Rom 12:1, KJV).

Away from Kucheng, on 27 July, an educated man who claimed to be a fortune-teller, Chang Chiu-chiu, known locally as "Long Finger-nails," had been sent by a secret society in Foochow to take control of the *Ch-ih-i-sai Ti* in the area. He had gained a superstitious hold over the movement's leaders and urged them to engage in a violent attack. Laying out three options—an assault on Kucheng, the village of Anchang, or the missionaries at Huasang, over three nights he rigged dice such that each time they fell on the third option. Their ultimate plan was to attack Kucheng and make it a base for a provincial rebellion in October. This was too much for some members of the *Ch-ih-t-sai Ti* movement. Several had family ties with the CMS Mission and did not agree with killing the foreigners who worked in it. One of these was the ousted leader who promptly sent a message to Robert Stewart that unfortunately arrived too late.

The following evening, 31 July, around one hundred men set out for the village. After bypassing Kucheng, they chose a back route to remain undetected by the villagers in Huasang. Carrying lanterns, the band followed behind a trumpet, drum, and red flag with *Ch-ih-t- sai Ti* insignia, bearing swords, spears, axes and other farming implements. On the way, a few of them began to drop off because they were having second thoughts about the proposed action.

Early morning on 1 August, while most of the adults were still asleep, Mildred and Kathleen Stewart went out to gather flowers for their brother Herbert's birthday picnic. They passed Annie Gordon who was reading her bible under the trees. The silence of the woods was suddenly broken by harsh shouts. At first the children thought they came from local workmen carrying materials. But when they saw spears, Mildred ran back towards the large house and Kathleen tried to hide in the grass. One of the attackers grabbed her by the hair but she managed to escape and ran after her sister. Brandishing swords and spears, several of the men rushed towards the house.

Hearing the girls scream for help, Nellie and Topsy were jolted awake and rushed to the front door. Disregarding her own safety, Nellie whisked them inside and slammed the door shut. Next, she helped the children hide under the beds. Meanwhile Topsy, concerned for the women in the second house, ran out the back door to alert them. Within seconds the first intruders burst into the living room. Still in her nightgown, Louisa Stewart came to her bedroom door and was immediately cut down by two attackers. As Robert stood dazed before her lifeless body, the leader of the group shouted; "We haven't come for your money but your life!" Three men then savagely hacked him to death with their swords. In the nursery next door, several other assailants turned upon the nanny. The intruders murdered Lena and attacked the baby she was trying to hide under her clothes.

Horrified at this, Nellie bolted the door of the boys bedroom, and stood resolutely before it to protect the children. A chant went up "Kill Nellie Saunders! Kill Nellie Saunders!" Two of the attackers viciously speared her and she fell writhing to the floor. Stepping over her dying body, they broke into the bedroom, looted the drawers, and pulled off all the bedclothes. They began beating Kathleen and slashed Mildred's knee. Escaping them, they ran into the nursery and pulled the mortally wounded baby from under the nurse's body. They then fled out the back door and hid in the bamboo wood.

Not knowing whether Nellie was alive or dead, Topsy rushed down the short slope between the two houses calling out to the other women, including Flora Codrington who had been staying nearby. Gathering in one of the bedrooms, they immediately knelt down and prayed. The men surrounded the house and kicked in the back door. At first, they didn't harm anyone but grabbed their possessions. They pushed the women, including Topsy, out the door, where the women found themselves surrounded by the rest of the mob. At this point an old man who had come up from the village pleaded desperately for their lives. The attackers conferred and then asked the missionaries for money. Since Topsy was the tallest, they assumed she was their leader. When they concluded from her answers that the women had nothing to give them, it was decided to bind and carry them off for ransom. But their leader, running down from the slaughter in the Stewart's house, abruptly intervened and ordered the women to be killed at once. Flora Codrington entreated the women to show courage, calling out "Sisters . . . we're all going Home together."[36] She told them to fall at the first blow in the hope of being left for dead. They were immediately attacked. Topsy was brutally speared in several places, the death blow piercing her eye into her brain. Annie Gordon's face and throat were mortally cut. Hessie Newcombe was so savagely struck that her head was almost severed. Flora Stewart was speared through the cheek and her lifeless body thrown down the hillside at the front of the house. Elsie Marshall was killed with her bible still in her hand. Flora Codrington, though her face was severely slashed, fell unconscious and pretended she was dead. In a side attack, one of the mob who had strayed from the group, wounded the American Mabel Hartford who was saved by the intervention of her Chinese servant.

---

36. Barnes, *Great Wall*, 143.

In a final act, the *Ch-ih-t-sai Ti* leader ordered the two houses to be burned, believing this would purify the land from the curse of foreign presence. As the fire gained strength the attackers shouted with delight. Outside the house, Kathleen realized it was up to her to rescue her younger brothers from the flames. She ran back inside, grabbed Herbert's hand and carried Evan out to where Mildred was hiding.

The Mission Houses after the Attack

The whole incident was over in around thirty minutes. First to arrive on the scene were some local villagers who, fearful for their own safety, had waited until the attackers had left. Then, a visiting CMS missionary, Rev Hugh Phillips, who had seen the flames from a residence on the next hill. One of the villagers led the children to Mabel Hartford's house. Later, with the help of Dr. Gregory who was also staying in the area, the charred remains and bodies of the victims were placed in coffins, and the survivors carried in chairs, for the three-day journey to Foochow. On reaching the Min River, three-year old Herbert died. From there, the rest were taken by launch, and a steamer provided by the American Consul, to Foochow. On 6 August the eleven victims were buried in the International Cemetery on Nantai Island. Each coffin contained a plaque with a name and an epitaph. On Nellie's coffin was engraved "Not counting their lives dear to them" and on Topsy's, "Jesus only." An overcrowded memorial service was conducted by Archdeacon Wolfe the following day.

THROUGH THE VALLEY OF THE SHADOW

Captured *Ch-ih-t-sai Ti* Leaders

經過死蔭的幽谷

News of the horrific incident ricocheted around the world. Within days the massacre was highlighted in major newspapers in the US, Australia, Britain, Ireland and China. Headlines included "Massacre in Huasang"[37], "Slaughter of Missionaries," "Appalling Atrocities," "Outrages at Kucheng," "Seven Lady Missionaries Butchered," "Christians Burned to Death." Diplomatic briefings and updates were regularly made to the relevant Government agencies. Public "indignation meetings" were held in places like Shanghai, Hong Kong, and London. Prayers encircled the world from Canada to New Zealand.

In Australia, the massacre was the subject of daily conversation in shops and workplaces, on buses and trams, in pubs and tearooms for several weeks . Editorial columns featured arguments for and against the sending of women, especially young women, to remote places in foreign lands. There were also debates about the rights and wrongs of imposing Christianity and Western culture on those with other traditions.

Within days, memorial services were held in capital cities, and some smaller towns, across denominations in Australia, England, Ireland and

---

37. This, for example, was the headline of *The New York Times*, 7 August 1895.

China. At these, Chinese who were present expressed their heartfelt sorrow and sympathy. Though understandably shocked and distressed on receiving the news, Eliza Saunders was remarkably composed. When interviewed by the press about sending young women to foreign countries, she replied that since culturally in China men could not approach females, who was going to rescue and help suffering women there? Asked whether she held any animosity towards the Chinese, Mrs. Saunders defended them by saying that the country should not be judged by the actions of a few any more than our own. When asked finally if, knowing what had happened, she would still allow her daughters to go to China, Eliza responded that if she had two more daughters they would also be freely given to the people of China.[38]

Partly influenced by foreign governments who had a presence in China, an official enquiry into the incident was soon set up in Foochow. The Commission's members visited and investigated the site, gathering detailed reports from survivors and those first on the scene. Meanwhile the Chinese military hunted down and arrested several dozen culprits. These men were brought to a highly-publicized trial in Foochow, whose proceedings over the next two months featured in major newspapers around the world. As this unfolded, political pressures were brought to bear by both British and Chinese authorities. Both sides agreed that severe penalties were justified, but some of the British desired wider reparations while some of the Chinese sought to restrict punishment to the *Ch-ih-t-sai Ti* leading perpetrators. Behind the scenes a compromise was finally reached. The most serious murderers, twenty-six in all, were beheaded and their bodies displayed at the entrance to the South Gate in Foochow as a warning to future terrorist acts. A further nineteen were banished or imprisoned for life; twenty-seven incarcerated for ten to fifteen years, and twenty for lesser periods.

While some thought the massacre would be a setback to missionary endeavor, paradoxically it turned out to be a significant stimulus to it. In Australia the impact was especially profound. Letters of sorrow and support poured into missionary societies working in China. A fund was set up for a permanent memorial to the Kucheng Martyrs—a striking Italian marble sculpture of an angel placed above their graves—to which people gave from all around the world. Offers to replace the women who died swelled the number of candidates in several missionary societies many times over. The three older Stewart boys, who were at boarding school in England when news came of the tragedy,

---

38. Barnes, *Great Wall*, 98. This was probably an echo of Hudson Taylor's well-known words: "If I had a thousand pounds, China should have it. If I had a thousand lives, China should have them. No! not China, but Christ. Can we do too much for Him?" See Broomhall, *Hudson Taylor*, II, 6.

all served in some capacity in China[39]: the three children who survived the attack also went to China as CMS missionaries. At Kucheng, a chapel was opened in the mission compound to commemorate those killed at Huasang, as well as a new Boys Boarding School in memory of Robert Stewart to which Chinese contributed liberally. The "massacre," as it came to be called, led to a revival of faith among local christians in Kucheng. Over the next few decades the city became one of the most vital centers of Christianity in the province and produced a number of influential church leaders, including its first Chinese Anglican bishop, Michael Chang. More than a century later, the authors have met young women in both Australia and China who were called to lifelong Christian service through the story of the Saunders sisters. In 1897, Mrs. Saunders herself finally went to Fukien with CMS, not as a housekeeper for her daughters but instead for other young women missionaries. Serving there without a furlough for nearly twenty years, in 1916 she was finally laid to rest alongside her girls.

Graves in International Cemetery, Foochow

As Nellie wrote in her diary, not long before the massacre: "Unless a grain of wheat falls into the ground and dies, it abides alone. But if it does die, it brings forth much fruit" (paraphrasing John 12:24, KJV).

---

39. After matriculating in Dublin, James Stewart went to Australia, graduated BA (Hons) at Sydney University in 1902, where he was a member of the Evangelical Union, studied Theology at Moore College, Sydney, in 1903, was ordained back in England in 1904, before heading to China.

2

Victoria Mannett

滿義德

University Teacher—Mianyang & Chengtu

Victoria Mannett

IN MID-APRIL 1911, AUSTRALIAN school teacher Victoria Mannett arrived in Mienchow, Szechwan Province, Western China.¹ Over the next few months

---

1. The earlier history of the CMS mission in Szechwan is summarized in the classic survey by Stock, *Church Missionary Society*, 325–28.

she found herself in an increasingly troubled situation. Protests, leading to violent riots, against the two-century old Qing Dynasty had broken out in the nearby capital of Chengtu. While she was learning the language, Victoria was assisting at the recently established Mienchow Girls Boarding School. With that city under imminent attack, the decision was made to send as many students home as possible. By 28 October, however, with food supplies running out, the city authorities shut the gates and prepared for the worst. The school was closed and a few days later the missionaries were ordered to evacuate to Chungking, 250 miles away on the Yangtze River, until the trouble subsided. Victoria's first opportunity to communicate this to her family back home was in the following detailed letter:

> On September 3rd we received the first serious news viz., that the shops were closing in defiance of the Viceroy's orders, and that the city was in open revolt. The university students were all dispersing to urge on others in other places to join them. Three days later, as soon as the students had left, the Viceroy ordered the city gate to be closed and then ordered soldiers to seize leaders of the League. Three were captured, and then the movement was thought to be checked . . . but it was more deep-set than anyone believed.
>
> Chengtu was in a dreadful state for days and rebellion was prevalent in all the cities nearby. The soldiers were called in from different parts to help, but most were really on the side of . . . the rebels or League members. These then began attacking the cities near the mountains. One after another fell into their hands after much fighting. In each place they opened the prisons and released the prisoners on condition that they would fight with them . . . The Viceroy and Consul-General advised all missionaries to restrict themselves to cities having direct river connection with Chungking, and on no account to do out-station work, but to keep within walled cities.
>
> On November 4th the first CMS party left Mienchow by two river boats for Chungking, hoping to stay there until things were quieter. At Chungking we found we belonged to a horde of people (even then rapidly increasing in number) called "refugees." As such, we could not stay in Chungking, therefore we then knew that Shanghai must be our destination. Another river boat, a trifle larger, was secured and we started as a party of eight CMS missionaries viz., two married couples, and four single ladies. A CIM party in another boat kept up with us most of the way. We were held up three times in one day by the rebels, but our boatmen were on the watch and ceased to row as soon as they were challenged.

Twice they were not satisfied by the men's answer, so we had to put into the shore. Some uniformed officers then came on board and when they found that we were only foreigners, they asked us why we did not have a flag. We made one and for the last two days before Ichang we were not challenged though we passed many rebel stations.

At Ichang, [500 miles further on] we found a large party of "refugees" waiting for the steamer, so our number was rapidly increasing. We boarded the steamer on Monday night, but our heavy load prevented us making quick progress . . . we were stuck on a sand-bank for three days . . . and did not really start again till Sunday. Grave reports were brought to us about the state of things near Hankow, but when we got near we heard that an armistice of several days had been declared. Then we seemed to know . . . why we had been allowed to be so long on the sand-bank . . . the city was a mass of ruins as we passed, with no sign of life anywhere and smoke still rising. We transhipped at Hankow and were able to go about in the foreign concession. On every side were signs of the recent fray and Red Cross boats were on the river resting a while after the dreadful last weeks. Gunboats of every nation were lined up. Calm after storm!"[2]

Finally, on 10 December, the flotilla landed in Shanghai, a trip of fifteen hundred miles overall. Victoria was relieved when her colleague from Melbourne, Mary Armfield, who had left the province in a later convoy, also arrived safely. Here the two women were able to share Christmas celebrations together. Being just the second and third CMA appointments to West China they had met a few times in Melbourne, then at the mid-year missionary conference in Szechwan, but spending this time together in Shanghai really cemented their friendship. A particular highlight was celebrating with the crowds on 1 January 1912 when Sun Yat-sen passed through Shanghai on his way to be inaugurated in Nanking as the provisional President of the new Chinese Republic. Towards the end of January, it became clear that ongoing instability in Szechwan meant it would be temporarily unsafe for them to return. Accommodation was found for the two of them in the CMS mission station in Ningbo, a major treaty port across the Yangtze Delta from Shanghai, where two other CMA teachers from Melbourne, twin sisters Eliza and Martha Clark, were based.

---

2. Her letter appeared in the *Hamilton Spectator*, 17 February 1912. Another eyewitness description of the evacuation by a CIM missionary is in Service, *China Memoir*. Attitudes of CMS missionaries to the Nationalist Revolution in southern China are described in Cunich, "Love and Revolution," 143–69.

Through the Valley of the Shadow
經過死蔭的幽谷

Victoria's journey to China had begun over ten years earlier. Growing up in suburban Melbourne she became a Christian through the ministry of her local Anglican church. After matriculating with honors in Mathematics at a prestigious private College, she qualified as a high school teacher and taught for a number of years in the city. In her early twenties Victoria experienced a growing conviction about the needs in China. A major influence at this time was reading the published letters of the Saunders sisters whose example and sacrifice greatly challenged her. During 1909 and 1910, Victoria enrolled at St Hilda's Missionary Training Home in Melbourne. While there she studied the history and culture of China and was delighted to learn she would be joining fellow Melbournian Mary Armfield in the province of Szechwan. Also that, an older son of Robert and Louisa Stewart, Rev James Stewart, was Warden of the Anglican Student Hostel at the new West China Union University in Chengtu and that his sister Mildred, who had escaped the massacre at Kucheng, and her husband were working among students with James.[3] Though Victoria knew that anti-missionary riots had taken place in the province in 1895, and further protests during the Boxer Uprising in 1900, this did not alter her resolve to go there. After leaving Melbourne in December 1910, she traveled via Shanghai to Chengtu, where she had the opportunity to meet the two Stewarts as well as Bishop Cassels, one of the widely-known "Cambridge Seven" whom she had read about during her study at St Hilda's. On reaching Mienchow she was accommodated at the Girls Boarding School while she began intensive language study of the local Mandarin dialect.

It was not until early October 1912, almost a year since their evacuation, that the Szechwan missionaries received word they could return. The reason this had taken so long lay in the unsettled politics of the province, particularly in Chengtu. For decades different warlords had fought for control of the city and, because the central authorities in Peking were so far away, often defied them. Local secret societies also sought to wield influence and university students occasionally agitated for reform. Groups of bandits ranged across the countryside, sometimes creating wider insecurity. As a result, it took much of 1912 for a positive attitude to the new Republic to consolidate in the city and for a measure of safety to be established in the region.[4]

---

3. James Stewart had arrived the year before and he was the one who had written to Victoria about the riots in Chengtu that begin this chapter.

4. For a broader perspective on Szechwan's seminal role in this see Hsu, *Modern China*, 465–74. A full account of this whole movement may be found in Lary, *China's Republic*, including its continuation in the Republic of Taiwan after 1949.

Victoria and Mary, along with their colleagues, began their six-week journey back to the province. As this was now free of conflict, they were able to enjoy its most scenic features, especially travelling through the majestic Three Gorges between Ichang and Chungking. The slow speed of the houseboat only accentuated the grandeur of the sheer cliffs surrounding them. There was also the thrill of the ride through dozens of surging rapids, alternating with the boat being hauled by large gangs of galley-men pulling ropes from the shore. They then had to cover the final two hundred and fifty miles on foot and by sedan chair. Luggage and food were carried by porters, who acted as protectors if they were confronted by robbers, and there was a cook to prepare their meals. Overnight stops were usually at inns which were often dirty, lacked privacy and sometimes shared with farm animals.

After passing through hilly country, they were delighted to see the great Chengtu plain, around half the size of France, stretching out before them. Thickly populated, it contained fifteen walled cities and fifty market towns as well as numerous temples and fortified hills. This plain, sometimes described as "Heaven on Earth," was the heart of the province and one of the great food-bowls of China. Its fertile soil, temperate climate and shelter provided by surrounding mountains, made it possible to grow a variety of crops all year round. Cash crops, like sugar cane, peanuts, cotton, tea, tobacco (and unfortunately opium) were a regular source of trade. Alongside this, the mining of metals used for manufacturing, as well as silver and gold, was becoming a growing industry.[5] Finally on 10 December the women arrived at the CMS headquarters in Mienchow. Mary continued on to the smaller city of Mienchu, forty miles further west, to resume her work among CMS Day Schools in the region.

With the completion of language study, Victoria was now able to focus on teaching at the Girls Boarding School. The boarders, aged from ten to nineteen, came primarily from other CMS schools in the district that only taught up to primary level. The local day students, aged from five to thirteen, did not continue beyond the age of puberty because a city law, among other things upholding child marriage, forbade girls to be out in the streets unchaperoned. Before coming to China Victoria envisaged her role purely as an evangelist, but soon realized that "she could reach the girls more easily through teaching"[6] in a school. To her great delight, at the start of the academic year in 1913, aged just thirty-two, Victoria was appointed Principal. Immediately she began to

---

5. This is drawn mostly from a reprinted Morrison Lecture by Mowll, "West China," 17–34, 118–20.

6. *Adelaide News*, 1 February 1924, 5.

implement the reforms in education proposed by the new Republican government in Peking.

Although the general political situation in the capital was temporarily somewhat settled, life in many of the smaller cities in the province remained unpredictable. As Mary Armfield wrote at this time:

> Our city was attacked by a big band of rebels. They liberated all the prisoners, robbed the Chinese, and looted everything they could lay their hands on. Fortunately, they remained faithful to their undertaking and left all the foreigners unmolested. But we in our mission were quaking with fear all the time. Our most anxious time was when during the rebel invasion of the city, 200 hundred Chinese women and children sought refuge under our roof. The poor creatures were frantic with terror. What could we do but give them the shelter they prayed for . . . We took them all in and hid them in every conceivable room and corner at our disposal. Fortunately, no suspicion was aroused, and, as I have said, the mission was left so severely alone that the fugitives were never discovered . . . We were glad when it was all over, and our big family of refugees could be safely out into the fresh air again.[7]

Not long afterwards, rebels also entered Mienchow, brandishing knives and guns close to the school. Concerned for her girls' safety, Victoria sought to negotiate with their leader, reminding him that the Mandarin was on his way with a force of three thousand soldiers. To her great relief, this strategy succeeded in extracting a promise of protection, at least for a time.[8]

Her first furlough in Melbourne was taken from April to September 1916. This time enabled Victoria to reassure family that she was safe and was enjoying the opportunity to help shape the future lives of girls in the province. Being home at the height of the First World War, she saw the tragic effects of news about so many soldiers being killed and wounded on the Western Front. A huge shock was hearing that James Stewart, who volunteered to serve as a Chaplain at the outbreak of war, had been shot while conducting a funeral service.

---

7. *Maryborough Chronicle*, 20 May 1914, 3.
8. *Church Missionary Gleaner*, 1 April 1915, 54.

Victoria (3rd row, 2nd from right) with other missionaries in Mienchow 1916

When Victoria returned to Mienchow at the end of 1916 the political situation in Szechwan had worsened. The strength of the Republican military forces had weakened and warlords were setting up separate governments with their own armies in a number of cities. This was not helped by Sun Yet-sen's successor Yuan Shikei's unsuccessful attempt to reintroduce the Imperial system with himself as Emperor. Altogether there were an estimated fifty thousand troops in Szechwan, and in 1917 Mienchow, now re-named Mianyang, was made the military headquarters of the republican forces. This made life in the city, including the school, more unstable, especially when it was taken over by a new revolutionary army seeking a more democratic model of national government. For a time, teaching in the school was disrupted when it became a refugee center for girls and prominent ladies in the city whose families sided with the central authorities in Peking.

The following year an Australian CMS missionary, Annie Jones, began teaching full time at the school and another, Alice Cooper, was preparing to do the same. In 1918, the growing activity of robbers in the district began to pose a threat to Victoria's students. Groups of brigands had long been a feature of life in Szechwan. These were largely comprised of rural hoodlums, petty criminals, demobilized or even unpaid soldiers. If caught they were often shot or beheaded, or absorbed into one of the local armies. Villagers and townspeople, especially those on the road, were the ones who suffered most at their hands. Now and again these bandits specifically targeted christian converts, breaking into their homes and taking their possessions. While they did not prevent missionaries from moving around, occasionally they forbad them to preach or hand out literature. These gangs were also known to kidnap ordinary Chinese, including children, demanding a ransom. As the number of girls coming to and from the school grew in numbers, Victoria had a growing concern for her students' safety.

At the start of first term, she wrote that due to "the troubled state of the country . . . the question of travelling and escort makes things very difficult just now. Since a great many of the girls have more than a day's journey from their homes to the school, I feel . . . a note of thanksgiving to God that . . . all 48 girls . . . came without the slightest hindrance. At the end of the term, all but 12 of the girls were able to return home in spite of all the dreadful things that have been happening."[9]

Drawing on her past experience at South Melbourne College, from the outset Victoria had begun training the most promising older students to assist teaching the younger ones. In 1919 she took this a step further by starting a small Senior School to prepare students for University. Victoria, already a valued member of CMS's Board of Education, contributed to the formation of the Western China Educational Union set up by five mission societies in the province. Its policies and practices for schools ultimately had an impact on educational reform elsewhere in China.

Each year since she had become Principal, the Girls School marked the anniversary of the Republic with a ceremony around the flag in the playground. This included an address by one or more of the teachers, as well as the national hymn and a prayer for the country. In early 1920, Victoria opened this up to a wider group of people, inviting the wives of the General and leading Civic Official, and other prominent women in the city. "We felt that we should help them know what true love for one's country meant . . . two women teachers spoke on 'Ideals for China' and 'Loving God is Loving One's Country.'"[10]

By the start of the new academic year in August 1921, enrolment at the school had grown from around forty to a hundred and fifty, equally divided between boarders and day students. Victoria estimated that around two-thirds were christian, many of whom were having a significant influence on members of their families. The school community also sought ways of preventing arranged marriages of young girls, often to much older men, by presenting a Christian view of marriage and preparing some older students to train for

9. Annual Letter, November 1918, 1.
10. Annual Letter, February 1920, 2.

the main professions and as church workers. Victoria viewed the role of her school as a vital contribution to the growth of both Christianity and education in China.[11]

During these years, as well as spending time with Mary when opportunity arose, Victoria had developed a friendship with a British CMS missionary. Dorothy Martin had arrived in Mienchu around the time Victoria returned from her furlough in Australia.[12] Her training and work was also in education and the two women found their progressive approach bonded them from the beginning. Though neither knew it at the time, in less than two years Dorothy was to marry the new Assistant Bishop in Szechwan, Dr. Howard Mowll from the UK who also became a close friend of Victoria.

經過死蔭的幽谷

In the months before she left Mianyang on furlough in early 1923, Victoria sensed that God had some new opportunity in mind for her return to China. Without having any clear idea what this might involve, or any proposal from CMS authorities in the province, she took a step of faith and resigned from the Girls School. This enabled the school to find a successor while she was away. This furlough offered the opportunity to speak at a variety of places, including St Paul's Anglican Cathedral in Melbourne. In her talks Victoria appealed for men and women to offer for service in China, stressing not only how much they could influence individuals but the wider society. Although there were ongoing protests among students, conflicts among warlords and violent attacks by bandits in China (including the recent murder of two of her CMS colleagues)[13], Victoria stressed that this was a providential moment for Christianity in that great nation's history.[14]

---

11. *Adelaide News*, 1 September 1924, 5. In her Annual Letter in November 1921, 2 that year, she described the school as occupying mentioned "a particular and important place in our work."

12. Dorothy had been born to CMS missionary parents in Foochow and was now returning to China as a missionary herself. She was already fluent in the language and had a good understanding of Chinese culture.

13. These were the Rev E. J. Watt and Rev R. A. Whiteside. See the report of the incident in the Sydney *Daily Telegraph*, 1 September 1923, 9 and an editorial on the memorial later set up in their honor in the *West China Missionary News*, May 1924, 1–2.

14. See the report on her address at St Paul's Cathedral, Melbourne, in *The Age*, 23 September 1923, 10 as well as list of speakers for 1924/5 at the Belgrave Heights Convention in its website at bhc.org.au. Also the lengthy interview in the *Adelaide News*, 1 February 1924, 5. In an informal conversation with students, Victoria declared that "she would not be surprised to learn that one day China would lead the world" (recorded in a

Victoria was deeply grateful to God that she was home when her mother fell seriously ill. She was able to care for her until she died several months later in December 1924. Just before her return to Szechwan in March 1925, she was invited to become a member of the faculty of Arts in West China Union University. The establishment of a Women's College made it the first co-educational tertiary institution within a range of two thousand miles. Victoria was the first Australian appointed to the faculty of the University. This was a wonderful vindication of the step of faith she had taken before leaving China. Though, according to the Secretary of CMS in Mianyang it was "a distinct compliment" to her, she felt a little daunted.[15]

Arriving in Chengtu via Mianyang in July 1925, Victoria marveled again at its impressive East Gate and massive city walls. A broad paved thoroughfare, bounded by trees and laced with canals, led to the city center. Often referred to as "little Peking," the capital was designed around a vice-regal palace, its own version of the Forbidden City. Dozens of traditional buildings reflected the architecture of different periods of Chinese history. Everywhere, however, there were signs of the new—electric lighting, motorized buses, public libraries and cinemas as well as post offices, telephone boxes and modern businesses.

The University was housed in an expansive park-like campus across the river from the South Gate and contained buildings that were a blend of Western and Chinese design. There were Departments of Arts, Science, Biology, Medicine and Dentistry. All these followed Western pedagogical methods, including the study of Chinese Language, History and Literature. Student activities were organized on self-governing, democratic lines, though the military in the city also used the University's grounds for parades. Students in general were averse to propaganda of any kind and were more likely to become interested in religion through social gatherings and casual conversation. Alongside the College chapel, each Sunday there was a united University Service geared to the interests of students that was well attended.[16]

On Victoria's arrival, repercussions of large student and worker protests in Shanghai, one involving two hundred thousand people, had reached the

---

letter from Georgina Bennett, Records on Victoria Mannett, 1.)

15. Rev. T. Caldwell, Records on Victoria Mannett, 1.

16. A detailed description of the founding and early development of the University may be found in Walmsley, *West China Union University*, 1974 and see also the article by Boreham, "Union University, 25–30. The importance and influence of Christian Higher Education Colleges in China is helpfully surveyed in Ng, "Rise and Development," 68–89 and, more expansively, in Lutz, *Christian Colleges*, 1971 as well as Bays and Widmer, *Cross-Cultural Communications*. A pictorial record of some of these institutions is provided by Erth and Johnston, *Hallowed Halls*.

Chengtu.¹⁷ It was the eve of a big demonstration taking the form of a strike by those employed by foreigners, including the university. Such was the build-up of resentment against Westerners, that being transported through the streets was extremely risky. As she writes: "Ignorant of the serious state of affairs I made my way in my open sedan chair through the city then out to the University but I was shielded round and "kept" so had no molestation."¹⁸

Group of Chinese Bandits

While she was settling into the Women's College dormitory, Victoria received word about a serious incident involving her friends Mary Armfield and the Mowlls. The background to this is contained in a circular letter from Bishop Cassels to all CMS and CIM missionaries in the province.

> The Chengtu Plain is rarely free from fighting and brigandage. In consequence, gambling and wine drinking are increasing, opium selling is carried on openly and the roads are lined with opium

---

17. The protests in Shanghai had been against the shooting of several Chinese workers by British police during a large strike in the city, which led to major disturbances in many provincial capitals.

18. Annual Letter, November 1925, 1. For a graphic depiction of what this was like, see the comparable scene in the film *The Painted Veil* (2006), based on the novel of the same name by W. Somerset Maugham.

dens. Illiteracy is rife among the rising generation owing to many of the country's schools having been so long closed. Men are more difficult to reach in their homes owing to the social upheaval. There is an absence of healthy public opinion. Wrong men are treated with honor. Just recently agitators from the south have invaded the Province, and the newspapers are filled with anti-foreign and anti-Christian propaganda. Is it any wonder that our members are few, and that progress seems so slow?[19]

The incident involved a group from Mienchu away together for their annual summer retreat to "Silverdale" in a mountain valley about ten miles from the city. There were nine of them in the party—including Mary Armfield and the Mowlls. According to the Bishop's account,[20] written soon afterwards:

> On the morning of Thursday, August 6th, we were awakened by the sound of rifle shots in quick succession close at hand. It was 5.30am. Half dazed, I remained in bed as the safest place in a room with so many big windows. Our dog barked, and suddenly stopped. Cries of 'Kill him!' "Strike dead!' could be heard. This was accompanied by the sound of feet on the stairs. The next minute the sickening sight of steel pikes splintering our bedroom door could be seen. By this time we had slipped on our coats, and I unbolted the door. The armed men outside pushed me downstairs at once. Our thumbs were quickly tied behind our backs. Near us were a row of workmen and two servants tied together. Our house had been the first to be attacked and they had not had time to escape. We were led to the neighbouring house to find the other party tied together with a rope round their necks.
>
> We were quickly led across the river . . . On the opposite bank we were untied and marched off into the hills between armed guards. Our last sight of our homes was to see the robbers streaming out with armfuls of our possessions and piling them into boxes . . . As the loads passed by we grabbed any useful clothing we could to supplement our scanty attire . . . Our captors avoided all roads and dragged us up and down steep hills all day . . . all day we were without food. We found a cup and slaked our thirst at mountain streams.
>
> As the afternoon wore on, we saw in the distance a grim looking mountain fortress with thick walls and narrow windows . . . We arrived just as it grew dark. As we passed up the narrow entrance

19. Cited in Loane, *Archbishop Mowll*, 93.
20. *North China Herald*, 3 October 1925, 12. A briefer account by Mary Armfield appeared in the Melbourne *Herald*, 28 October 1925, 10.

we saw that the robbers had lighted a great fire at which they were cooking their meat. In its light we could see what was left of our possessions in disordered array in a large room. They had been well picked over. We went supperless to bed except for a drink of water . . . The ladies packed themselves on top of a cupboard for the night and had not even room to turn.

So began two weeks of forced walks among the hills and valleys, often in grim and rainy weather, with overnight stays in farms, ruined buildings or in the open. The captives often went without food or water, and sometimes even blankets on cold evenings. They often walked in circles and crossed rivers in makeshift crafts. At times fever struck a member of the group and once they spent the night with coffins of murdered captives in the next room. The group was constantly watched, had guns waved at them and, on one occasion, a bandit brandished his sword at the only child in the party. Despite this, according to Mowll: "It was our constant prayer that by word, deed, and bearing we might influence these evil men for good. We had one pocket testament with psalms that was a never failing source of comfort to us."

Finally, after another week on the road, through some negotiations with locals, there was a break through and the bandits disappeared. Soldiers arrived to escort them back to Mienchu. On the way, the streets in every village were lined with people cheering them on and in the city the chief official had prepared a feast. Their release was due to the combined efforts of the Magistrate in Chengtu and CMS representatives who arranged a payment that was much less than the bandits originally demanded. Howard Mowll's hope was that, as a result of this incident, new doors would be opened up for the Gospel and bring them and the people more closely together.

Throughout this harrowing experience, Victoria was deeply anxious for her friends, especially as there was no news about their fate for nearly a month. She was also aware that, if Mianyang had still been her base, she would probably have been among the group captured.

When, in August, Victoria began teaching in the University, large student rallies inciting violence against foreigners were still taking place. Her courses, taught across different departments, were in Education, Science and Scripture. This was only the second year that women, including six girls from CMS mission schools, were allowed to study at the University. Her other responsibilities included being a faculty representative on both the Women's College Committee and University Senate.

Administration Building, West China Union University

In October, outside agitators stirred up campus protests against a naval encounter between the British and Chinese on the Yangtze River. This resulted in the University being shut down for nearly three weeks. Victoria commented that: "nationalistic feeling has taken a strong leap forward during the upheaval and we are facing a new state of things entirely. This has been looming for some time but is now right upon us.[21] Consequently, before the next term began, Westerners in the province were ordered by the British Consul, as they had been in 1911, to evacuate to Shanghai.[22]

As conditions did not improve in Szechwan, Victoria was encouraged by Bishop Mowll to go on furlough, arriving in Melbourne at the end of May 1926. During the next six months she spoke at more than eighty meetings across Victoria. These aimed at educating Australian audiences towards a more realistic understanding of what was happening in China, talking about the positive things happening through christian students in her university, and lamenting the fact that CMS had not been able to respond to the need for helpers in the sphere of Christian Higher Education in China. Without this assistance, her view was that China was in danger of becoming Communist and this would only be prevented by students seeing another alternative.

Victoria returned to China in 1928 but was delayed in Hong Kong waiting for the situation in Chengtu to stabilize. In the meantime, she was seconded to teach at St Stephen's College but was pleased to get back to Chengtu the following year in time for Howard Mowll's installation as Anglican Bishop

21. Annual Letter, November 1925, 4.
22. Annual Letter, December 1926, 2.

for the whole of West China, with the Chinese Bishop C. T. Song as his assistant. Delighted to resume teaching in the University, Victoria began holding: " . . . open house on Sundays for lunch and discussion, as well as tea and games on Saturdays, with students"[23] . . . "Many of these young women are far away from their homes, and those first years in new surroundings are fraught with great possibilities for good or ill: hence the need for someone who can be a friend and adviser is a special one."[24]

Women Education students at the University

It was good to see more students coming to the University from non-Christian schools and she also worked with the University Extension Centre to teach classes in other parts of the province. In Victoria's opinion the University was gaining greater respect in the city and there was a growing recognition of Western, including christian, contributions to society. The first women were now graduating from the University and taking up positions as teachers, nurses and church workers in the province. In all her work among the Chinese, she sought to live by the maxim that missionary work required "sympathy, insight, tact and was impossible for anyone with a superiority complex."[25]

23. Annual Letter, August 1930, 7.
24. Mannett, "Girl Students," 116.
25. As later expressed in a talk reported in the Hobart *Mercury*, 12 February, 1934, 2. On Chinese Christians increasingly taking responsibility in these years, see Dorothy Mowll, *Armidale Express*, 28 September 1934, 10.

Through the Valley of the Shadow
經過死蔭的幽谷

The early 1930s were marked by continuing unsettled conditions in and around Chengtu. Inflammatory remarks in a Russian-owned newspaper in the city triggered further student protest that led to intimidation of the University's President and destruction of some property. In the countryside, bandit raids on land and pirate attacks on rivers became bolder and more rampant. The Mowlls were again affected by this. As they were returning along the Yangzte from another province with some missionary recruits, their boat was halted by several official-looking men.

> Six men in long gowns and armed with revolvers came on board and began to search their bags. They thought for a moment that they were just arrogant officials making a custom inspection, but that supposition was soon dispelled. The men were all very excitable and began to demand silver. When there was no response they tried to find out where the supposed treasure was concealed. One man fired two shots close to the Bishop and then clubbed him with his revolver. He was stabbed in the back and his wife was struck on the head. They were bleeding freely.[26]

After stealing some jewelry and clothing, the pirates disappeared into the failing light. The Bishop was seriously wounded, but after Dorothy dressed his wounds they were able to resume their journey. At the next wharf arrangements were made for a car to collect them and get medical help.

Towards the end of 1932 the military situation in the province also drastically worsened. The armies of three Generals were vying for control of Chengtu. The conflict began with the first air raid over the city, followed by fierce ground combat. At the time Victoria, who was staying in the Bishop's House during the Mowll's absence, heard the fighting coming closer. As she was securing the building, Bishop Song and his family, along with two other missionaries, arrived seeking refuge from the conflict.

In the city, each army sought to fortify its section against the others. Barricades were built out of torn-up road pavings. Soldiers occupied shops, businesses and warehouses. On 16 November, severe fighting broke out in the streets. Rifles and machine guns, mortars and hand-grenades, as well as long-range artillery, were all used freely in crowded, narrow streets and broader thoroughfares. Houses were demolished and thousands of civilians caught in the cross-fire.

---

26. Loane, *Archbishop Mowll*, 121. The event was also reported in Brisbane's *The Telegraph*, 20 February 1932, 16.

Victoria Mannett

As the fighting moved over the river, the Diocesan compound was taken by soldiers of the 24th Army. Hearing their advance, Victoria and the others moved to the most protected part of the house. Since it was a two-storey building, with a commanding view of the University grounds, soldiers entered it and made it their base. The opposing Army took up positions across the University and a fierce battle ensued. Hiding under tables and behind cupboards in the Bishop's House, Victoria and the others felt the impact of heavy shells falling outside. As the battle became more intense, hand-grenades were lobbed into the house, and bullets fired from the roof of the nearby Student's Hostel. Though several soldiers in the house were killed or wounded, the non-combatants sheltering under cover were not harmed. It was a frightening experience, especially as the battle continued the whole day into the evening. As an observer recorded:

The Student Hostel across from the Bishop's House

The soldiers in the Bishop's House looted it entirely, breaking open every cupboard, draw and box, and taking everything they wanted, leaving the remainder in a terrible state of disorder and ruin . . . They tried to take the Bishop's car, breaking open the garage door to the street, but Miss Mannett, Bishop Song and Mrs Kao persuaded them to desist and they did the car no damage. As you will easily imagine, this was a veritable reign of terror for all the people in the compound. Miss Mannett was the only foreigner.

Her courage and patient endurance, and those of Bishop Song and family are simply beyond praise ... Each night [since] there has been heavy fighting all around us. Aeroplanes came over the city on Saturday and Sunday and dropped a few bombs but not near.[27]

A peace was finally patched together but stability was not fully restored until the 29th Army left the city to counter a Communist force invading the north of the province. One of the positive by-products of the fighting in Chengdu was a number of soldiers expressing strong interest in Christianity as a result of meetings held throughout the battle in their barracks.

It took time for Victoria to begin coming to terms with all that she has been through. As well as experiencing constant fatigue, her nerves were triggered by any sudden loud noise. Evenings were the worst as she struggled to sleep and overcome recurring nightmares. Alongside her heavy teaching load, many committee meetings and student ministry, Victoria was also asked to undertake additional duties—giving lectures to theological students, making regular visits to Mianyang to train teachers, offering short courses in educational methods around the Diocese, and mentoring itinerant evangelists. A respite from this round of responsibilities was offered by Howard Mowll's request that she accompany Bishop Song and Mr. Wu, Principal of the Boys Middle School in Mianyang, on a visit to England. While there, for three months from the beginning of September, she advised CMS on work in Women's Colleges in China and helped Mr. Wu settle into Ridley College, Cambridge, for a year's theological study. This visit provided Victoria with a complete change of environment as well as an opportunity to meet some relatives for the very first time before a year's furlough in Australia.

Sharing Christmas and New Year with passengers on the boat home, she arrived in Melbourne in January 1934. After fulfilling some initial speaking engagements that had already been arranged, CMS Medical Officers examined her and recommended three months complete rest, starting immediately. In the second half of the year, renewed in energy, she was invited to visit University Women's Colleges in Melbourne and Sydney. This gave her opportunity to meet up with the Mowll's who, since had recently moved to Sydney where Howard was now the Anglican Archbishop. Wherever she went, Victoria's talks were of interest to journalists who reported in detail on her assessment of Chinese culture and politics.[28]

---

27. See the Melbourne *Argus*, 15 April 1933, 7. Further accounts of the battle occur in "The Fighting," 1–2 as well as brief reports in the *Church Missionary Outlook*, March 1933, 57–58, and the *CMS Home Gazette*, May 1933, 75.

28. In Melbourne's *The Age*, 12 January 1934, 6, and *The Argus*, 12 January 1934, 10.

It was not until November that she was approved by CMS to return to Szechwan. The Women's College was celebrating its tenth anniversary, and the fact that now almost one-third of the total student body in the University was female. Feeling that her pioneering work there was largely complete, Victoria was hoping for a position that would free her to act as an educational consultant to the wider Diocese. It was an answer to prayer when CMS appointed her to Mianyang as advisor to the now Rev Wu at the Boys Middle School, and the following year to the Chinese Principal of the Girls Boarding School, with time to travel and speak throughout the province.

When Victoria arrived in mid-March, despite the presence of Communist forces in the north east of Szechwan, life in the city appeared "fairly normal."[29] On the first of April, however, as the "Red Raiders" were becoming an imminent threat, orders came from the Bishop for the two schools to prepare for possible evacuation due to military forces in the city bracing for significant conflict.

Overnight all students and staff who lived in the city or nearby villages were instructed to return home. This left around sixty boys, girls and remaining teachers. The two Principals, Victoria and staff decided to take this remnant "on the road" to safer places in the south. The next morning further orders came to move out immediately, leaving only two hours to hurriedly prepare. Each student was encouraged to wear as much clothing as possible so that they would keep warm at night. A few carts were packed with provisions and cooking implements for several days. Medical supplies, blankets, lanterns, books and notepads were added.

Victoria's past experience of two major evacuations was indispensable both in preparing the students and helping plot a route for the journey. Instead of taking the main road, they traveled a circuitous way that gave them more contact with local christians who could potentially help them. Though this plan exposed them to greater threat from bandits, it was felt that the size of the group and number of adults was worth the risk. After five days they reached the town of Sintu, which had a small missionary compound, fifty miles away. There they were able to stay for a week and even hold makeshift classes.

Further orders then arrived that the band should proceed to Chengtu. However, since all Western civilians had been ordered to evacuate the city, Victoria was asked to find safety elsewhere. Though it was hard to leave her students and colleagues at such an unsettled time, she promised to return as soon as the situation stabilized. She then contacted some American Methodist friends from her West China University days working in a small town out of the danger zone in the mountains. They responded immediately, inviting her

---

29. Annual Letter, August 1935, 2.

to stay with them. It took her five days by boat to reach Taichow safely. Victoria spent the next seven weeks there, helping out by teaching some advanced classes as well as in other practical ways. Finally, on 4 June, the officials in Chengtu declared the Communist danger over and Victoria was delighted to rejoin the travelling school in the capital for the closing weeks of the academic year. It was not long before she and her fellow teachers were able to return to Mianyang.

The situation in the city changed again in the second half of 1937. The Japanese, emboldened by their earlier victory over the Chinese in Korea, had occupied Manchuria in 1933, and now began attacking adjacent provinces in the north and major cities along the coast. After Shanghai, and then Nanking, fell to their advances, Chiang Kai-shek decided to make distant Szechwan his base for fighting them. Academics escaping the Japanese from leading cities in the east, also began to flock to Chengtu, turning it for a time into the most vibrant intellectual center in the country.

Towards the end of 1937, Mary Armfield had arrived at the Boys School in Mianyang to work as Victoria's assistant and reduce her workload. However, after a few months Mary's health began to deteriorate. She was increasingly suffering from endemic fatigue, fever, dysentery and weight loss. It became clear that she needed specialist medical help that was not yet available in China. CMS then gave the word that Mary should return to Australia. Since she needed a carer for the long journey, Victoria was seconded to do this. Though her furlough was not due for another two years, and she felt the loss of having to "leave my Chinese co-workers who are now facing especially difficult problems—spiritual, political and social,"[30] she was ready to do this. Describing her own struggles at this time, Victoria wrote: "I confess I had been feeling the strain of the abnormal conditions existing (for me) in our station but that had not kept me from the service which was my privilege to give."[31]

經過死蔭的幽谷

On 10 October the two women went by air from Chengtu to Kunming, where Mary was allowed to rest for a few days, and then on by rail to Haiphong. After another short break, during which Canton fell to the Japanese, they embarked on a steamer for Hong Kong, resting there for a few days before boarding a ship that reached Melbourne on 28 November.

---

30. Annual Letter, August 1938, 30. She accepted CMS's decision to return home with Mary after hearing a talk on "Never Challenge the Umpire": by a Chinese Christian.
31. Further to Annual Letter, November 1938, 2.

Victoria (middle) with Mary (right) returning to Australia

Back in Melbourne Mary was properly diagnosed with tropical sprue and with medical help and rest gradually her health improved. In April 1939, CMS gave Victoria an excellent medical report and began making arrangements for her return to West China. Due to the ongoing war with the Japanese, they heard back from Szechwan that this would be too dangerous. While waiting for better news, Victoria continued to educate Australians about the situation in China.[32] For six months she worked as Mission Education Secretary at Holy Trinity Church Adelaide and, probably at Archbishop Mowll's urging, from the beginning of 1941 as CMS Branch Education Secretary in Sydney.

Later that year, Victoria and the Mowlls were delighted when Bishop Song was able to make an unexpected friendship tour to Australia. The three of them welcomed him when his ship docked, and they spent many hours talking over old times at Bishopscourt where he was staying. Song also insisted a get together with "Miss Mannett, Miss Armfield and Miss Cooper [who] are my 'three sisters' in Australia."[33] At one of his many civic welcomes the four of them sang the opening hymn in Chinese. During Bishop Song's visit he spoke in churches, theological colleges and universities, met with many business,

---

32. See her addresses in the *Murray Pioneer*, 10 October 1940, 16 and, later, the *Port Lincoln Times* 17 October 1944, 1 where she stressed "Australia's great opportunity to play a part in the rise and development of that country."

33. "Letter from Bishop Song," *Diocese of Western China*, January 1942, 11–12, 6–12.

educational and political leaders, and dined with the Governor General. He proved to be an impressive ambassador for Christianity in China.[34]

Towards the end of that year, with the war between Japan and China continuing to deepen, CMS informed Victoria that there was no possibility of her returning to Szechwan. While understanding the reasons for this, she continued to long for the people who had been such an important part of her life for nearly three decades. In the following years, "she gave herself unsparingly to the work of the Home Base. She was a valued member of ... the governing body of St. Hilda's and of the West Asia Regional Committee of the Federal Council. She also represented the Branch on the National Missionary Council ... For a time she also edited the Fellowship of Prayer and the Victorian section of the CMS Australia Report."[35]

Victoria died on 17 September 1958 and her ashes were interred in the Gardens of Remembrance at St Mary's and St Margaret's, Caulfield. However, the legacy of her pioneering work in Szechwan continues in the province to this day. Her school in Mianyang is now the leading Middle School in the city and the university in Chengdu, today Sichuan University, is one of the leading campuses in China.

In recording her passing, CMS Victoria noted that: "She loved the Chinese people and following Archbishop Mowll's visit to China in 1956 he had the pleasure of telling her that there was 'no former missionary whom the Chinese more frequently asked after than herself'. During her time in China there were periods of great political strife and consequent danger and in the midst of this her calm courage and faith were outstanding."[36]

---

34. Bishop Song also met our grand-aunt, a retired missionary from Fukien Province and friend of the Mowlls. He wrote: "I was deeply touched by being invited to lunch with Miss Newton, a returned missionary from China, who is 75 years old and lives entirely alone in her house which is situated in a mountain district. She is so filled with Christ that one felt as if one had met an angel on the mountain. We had prayer together." (*Diocese of Western China,* January 1942, 11.)

35. Cole, *Servants,* 90.

36. Resolution of the General Committee of CMS Victoria, 1 December 1958.

3

Martha and Eliza Clark

滿義德—閔愛理

School Principals—Ningpo & Shanghai

Martha and Eliza Clark

IT WAS JUNE 1925. Just as classes were finishing for the day, from her office Eliza Clark heard loud voices coming up the street towards St Catherine's School. Peering out the window she saw about fifty senior girls from government schools who had crossed the bridge from the city and were shouting to her students: "Don't be lackeys of the foreigners and running dogs of the

Imperialists!" On hearing this, Eliza and the Chinese Matron went outside to meet the group. Their leaders demanded that they close the school tomorrow and allow its students to take part in a large protest meeting outside the nearby British Consulate. Five days earlier in Shanghai, fifteen university students had been arrested for agitating against poor working conditions in a Japanese cotton factory. This led to some thirty-five strikes throughout the city and to an even larger protest where ten people were shot by British-controlled local police. In the wake of this, public anti-foreign demonstrations, primarily involving students, supported by academics, sprang up almost overnight in various Chinese cities.[1]

After expressing her concern about this tragic occurrence, Eliza explained that, because there was real potential for violence at the meeting tomorrow, it was not possible for her to give students permission to attend. Not to be put off, the visitors milled around the school gates for the next two hours, distributing pamphlets to day students who were on their way home and appealing to boarders to attend the Rally. Around 5pm some senior government school boys, led by a very vocal middle-aged man, arrived on the scene. Belligerently confronting the Matron, he demanded to come into the office but she refused him entrance. When it became clear that this bullying manner was not going to work, he declared: "We'll be back with reinforcements tomorrow morning to break down the gate and take the girls with us." He then signalled to the crowd to disperse.

As soon as they left, Eliza ran to tell her sister Martha in the Women's Bible School next door what had just happened. They decided to call a little "war council" consisting of the two of them and a couple of senior Chinese staff. The male Property Manager mentioned that a few young men were left hanging around the gate to keep a watch on any attempted movements. This reminded them of an incident the previous year when soldiers fired at each other in the street outside and a few girls were nearly shot in the crossfire. At the time the Matron suggested that if any emergency like this ever happened again, the students could be smuggled out by a side-door hidden from the road. With the assistance of staff members, this would have to be done under cover of night and students then escorted through back streets to their homes. They all agreed this was the best plan. As for girls who came from outside the city, Martha proposed that they be secretly housed in her Women's School at the far end of the mission compound. Working steadily through the night, it took till dawn to complete this covert operation.

---

1. On the development of student movements in Shanghai see Wasserman, *Student Protest* and on their further history and influence see Lutz, *Chinese Politics*.

Martha and Eliza Clark

The next morning the government school students returned, this time in greater numbers and with provocative banners. Banging drums and chanting for the students to come out, they climbed on the front walls of the school and started pressing against the gates. The Property Manager shouted from inside the building: "There is not a single girl here—our students were so distressed by what happened yesterday that they have all gone home!" Having lost face by the failure of his plan, the leader moved the group on to join the main body of protesters, where around 3000 students were already gathering and shouting: "Down with the British Empire!"[2]

經過死蔭的幽谷

It took the sisters several days to fully reflect on all that had happened and what it meant for the future of their work. They agreed that this was the most politically troubled and dangerous year in Ningpo since arriving some twenty years earlier. Before leaving Australia, the Clarks knew the possible cost of missionary service in China. In 1895, when they were just sixteen, both girls had been challenged by the story of the Saunders sisters and understood that facing conflict was an inevitable part of their call.

The Clark sisters were born into a well-to-do Melbourne family on 9 September 1878. They were raised in a home where education was valued. Their businessman father, a graduate of Cambridge University, sent all of his six children to leading schools, the boys to Hawthorn Grammar and the girls to Tintern Grammar. When Martha and Eliza were eight, he died suddenly of a heart attack, leaving his wife at the age of thirty to cope with six children under ten. Coupled with this, the 1890s Depression saw the family also lose many of its assets and social standing.

Their mother found "the adjustment to a more frugal lifestyle very difficult. Used to many servants, the upbringing of the children became too much for her, and she took to 'retiring' upstairs and seeking solace in brandy."[3]

These experiences of loss drew Martha and Eliza—whose nicknames were Minnie and Lyda—even closer together. As identical twins, they were able to communicate with each other without speaking and knew intuitively when the other wanted help. They tended to act as one person and often spoke in the plural. As the eldest girls they took responsibility for running the household and keeping the family together.

---

2. This account is reconstructed from Eliza Clark, Annual Letter, October 1925, augmented by her comments in St. Columb's Newsletter, September 1925, 4.

3. This comes from the brief biographical thesis by the twins's relative Alison Hart, "Unshakeable Faith," 2.

From an early age the sisters had a strong link with their local Anglican church, St Columb's Hawthorn, and its minister, Rev C. H. Nash, a strong promoter of missionary work. A large number of Chinese came to church services and bible studies, which the girls also attended. In their teens Martha and Eliza both taught Sunday School and became increasingly involved in CMA's Gleaners' Union, especially after the massacre in Kucheng that "sent a shudder of horror through the community."[4]

After matriculating from Tintern Grammar, Martha taught Scripture at local government schools for several years. Their mother's early death from alcohol in 1902 finally freed her to apply to the CMA for work in China. On her acceptance in 1903, she studied bible and theology with Rev Nash, and then took classes in church history, mission geography and first aid at St Hilda's Training Home.

Even though Eliza knew that her sister's decision would change her life considerably, she trusted God to look after them both. Finally, on Tuesday 28 October 1904, Martha left Melbourne for Ningpo, just south of Shanghai, in Chekiang province. Never having travelled outside Australia before, she was pleased that returning CMA Victorian missionary teacher, Isabel Hughes, would accompany her.

Ningpo was one of the original Chinese treaty ports opened up to the West and became the headquarters of Anglican work in the region from the 1840s. It became a key base for both CMS and CIM as well as several American and Canadian missionary societies.[5] CMS had a well-established compound in the foreign concession near the "Bridge of Boats," over the Yong river, just outside the city. This housed three schools which were the most advanced Anglican educational institutions in the province—Trinity College (which contained a Preparatory School and small Theological Seminary), St Catherine's Girls School, and a Women's Bible School to train rural evangelists and teachers. Alongside these was a Hospital, Chapel and several staff residences.[6]

---

4. Op. cit., 4.

5. On the establishment of CIM work in Ningpo, see Broomhall, *Hudson Taylor*, especially Vols. 2 and 3.

6. A summary of the developing CMS work in Chekiang province may be found in Norris, *English Church Expansion*, ch. 8.

"Bridge of Boats" Ningpo

Ningpo had come into prominence during the seventh century Tang dynasty and was famous for traditional Chinese furniture-making, tea growing, silk-weaving and, more recently, cotton industries. Its port was one of the three busiest in the country. The city experienced hot, humid summers and cold, drier winters, with occasional falls of snow. It possessed China's oldest library, dating back to the eleventh century, which contained handwritten copies of Confucian classics and rare local histories. "Filled with small houses, packed so closely together and numerous graves, small streets and canals, [the city] was enclosed within a wall about fifteen feet high that took well over an hour to walk around."[7]

For the first two years, Martha was engaged in learning the Ningpo dialect, a form of Wu Chinese. Staying at the CMS Hospital, she also helped care for sick girls. Letters to her sister back home expressed her frustration at not being able to get out into the countryside to work amongst the people. Meanwhile Eliza felt a growing conviction that God was also calling her to China. This was not just because she was "finding the separation from her older and more adventurous twin very difficult."[8] If she was accepted for missionary

---

7. Hart, "Unshakeable Faith," 7.
8. Hart, "Unshakeable Faith," 7.

work, Eliza knew that her chance of being placed with Martha was very slim indeed.

She enrolled for a year's study at St Hilda's in September 1905, not knowing where she would finally end up. On her arrival in November 1906 she was appointed to Hangchow, an historic ninety miles north-west of Ningpo. While learning the local dialect, she assisted the Bishop's daughter in the smaller school there. Dr. G. E. Moule, brother of the renowned Professor Handley Moule in Cambridge, was one of the founding missionary figures in the province: his two brothers, four children and nephew all served in Chekiang.[9]

Despite the initial decision to separate the two sisters, within a year the missionaries in Ningpo argued that it would be more effective for Eliza to teach there so Martha could be freed for pastoral work among women in the countryside. Their view that, for these twins, one plus one equals three, eventually won the day! Martha itinerated largely by boat on the province's rivers and canals. She spent about a month in each of its six districts visiting enquirers, encouraging scattered christians and holding informal Bible and English classes in their homes.

Returning from a furlough in Australia in late 1911, Martha was present when the new Chinese Republic was inaugurated under Sun Yat-Sen. In Ningpo, due to the attitude of civic authorities and leading businesspeople, this change took place with little public disturbance or antagonism to foreigners.[10] Not long after her arrival, she was appointed Principal of the Women's Bible School. Though Martha was initially disappointed that this would only allow time for itinerating once a year, she soon realized how much more village women could learn in three-month long courses away from the distractions of: "babies, neighbors, chickens, household cares etc. The women were taught Romanized writing, reading and general subjects as well as their Bible studies, with the intention that after several terms they could return to their villages and begin small day schools for local children."[11]

After completing additional language study in Ningpo dialect, Eliza was appointed as Acting Principal at St Catherine's School. It was during her furlough from late 1911 to late 1912, that Martha welcomed Victoria Mannett and Mary Armfield to Ningpo while they were waiting for the situation in Szechwan to settle so they could return. Back home in Australia, Eliza she spent three months at Melbourne Girls Grammar, learning various aspects of

---

9. His grandson, C. F. D. Moule, who the Clark sisters knew as a young child in Hangchow, became an internationally celebrated Professor of New Testament in the UK at Cambridge University.

10. The reasons for this are explored in detail by Chen, *China's Network Revolution*.

11. Hart, "Unshakeable Faith," 7.

running a boarding school. Soon after her return to China, Eliza was named Mistress of the boarding house at St Catherine's and, just over two years later, Principal of the school. By 1919 she had managed to elevate the educational standards of St Catherine's so that it received secondary school status and was therefore now able to take over the work of training teachers from Trinity College. Along with their missionary colleagues, the sisters also sought to improve the conditions of Chinese women by teaching them basic hygiene and medical care, and by opposing child marriage and foot binding which, though no longer legal in China, were still widespread in the countryside.

Trinity College in the CMS compound

Martha and Eliza continued in these roles until the mid-1920s. Through this period, like most missionaries both women suffered occasional bouts of malaria and pneumonia, and experienced natural disasters like typhoons, one of which blew down the heavy walls of their compound. Letters from home about the unexpected death in 1919 of their younger and only sister, Louise, deeply affected them, but they were grateful for the time they had spent with her while on their second furloughs twelve months earlier.

Until the early 1920s, the sisters were not seriously troubled by expressions of anti-foreign resentment or outbreaks of armed conflict. Initially the May Fourth demonstrations in Shanghai objecting to China's treatment in the Treaty of Versailles after the First World War, made only a small impact in Ningpo. Over the next few years, student protests increasingly took place against both traditional Confucian and imported Christian influence, particularly in education. These were considered reactionary philosophies that were holding China back from modernising. In late 1921 Eliza wrote about the after-effects of these protests, noting how literature was being distributed that could poison the minds of Chinese youth.[12] From 1922 student protest increasingly focused on christian educational institutions, urging their reform to fit the aspirations of a modern state. Two years later an organized movement developed in Shanghai and in 1925 the first anti-Christian society was inaugurated in Ningpo. As a consequence of the May Thirtieth incident involving police shootings in Shanghai, the movement became increasingly strident and nationalistic.[13] This formed the background to the student demonstrations at St. Catherine's and Trinity College described earlier.

經過死蔭的幽谷

The student demonstrations resulted in both schools closing ahead of the summer vacation. Eliza feared that otherwise her students might be forced to sign documents stating that they would not return to the school. Around this time, the sisters were experiencing a change of attitude towards Westerners. In the streets it was not uncommon to hear people calling out "Go home foreigners!" and "Strike them to death!" For Eliza and Martha it was a relief to go to CMS's summer conference and relax in the Kuling mountains, east of Hangchow. When St Catherine's re-opened in early September, there was around a 20 percent drop in enrolments, mostly girls from non-Christian homes.

In the following year, challenges arising from student protests for educational reform were superseded by the increasing threat of military conflict. Southern forces led by Chiang Kai-shek were moving up from Canton in an attempt to revive the failed Republic against Northern forces more interested in simply retaining power.[14] At first, fighting in the province took place at a distance from Ningpo. By the beginning of 1927, however, Chiang Kai-shek's forces were closing in on the city. Eliza describes the confusing series of events that followed.

12. Annual Letter, November 1921, 1–2.
13. On this whole development see the detailed treatments in Chen, *May Fourth Movement* and Lutz, *Chinese Politics*.
14. See further Hsu, *Modern China*, 523–31.

Ningpo belonged to the Southerners for about a fortnight, the pupils getting more disturbed and troubled as to how they should get home. So we were advised to close the school in the beginning of January. Then the Northerners came into power and again we had great hopes of reopening the school after the Chinese New Year.

Then came the Northerners defeat. The people were greatly afraid of the defeated soldiers—they feared looting and worse—we took our remaining girls to the Women's School compound which is rather hidden among other buildings.

When the victorious Southerners came they gave no trouble and we hoped for peace. But soon rumours began to get about and we were all advised to send one box [of personal possessions] to Shanghai for fear we had to leave with little notice . . .

Then we received notice from the local authorities that we were not to have practices such as reading the Scriptures and prayers—there were six other points including "Pupils to have freedom to form societies, to hold discussions and print articles in the press." It was decided it was impossible to reopen the school until these matters were resolved.[15]

These reforms resulted from the earlier May Thirtieth student movement focusing not just on general educational reform but on specific rights for students in all schools. However, before there could be any further discussion with the local authorities about these requirements, in March the British Consul ordered all missionaries to evacuate to Shanghai. There the women linked up with missionaries from other provinces, including Victoria Mannett and Mary Armfield from Szechwan. For the next seven months the Clark sisters were housed in a secular International School. While there, they were engaged in teaching and evangelism in English to students that were mostly from ex-patriate families. Their facility in Chinese also enabled them to assist an American deaconess in a local orphanage and refugee center.

Martha's correspondence reveals concern at what could potentially be lost during their absence. "To think of Ningpo at the moment seems the demolition of [the] work of years yet we cannot be discouraged for God reigns and out of all the confusion I believe a purified church will arise."[16]

At points during their stay, violence broke out in the streets, reminding them how volatile China was at the moment. Their time in Shanghai was interspersed with a disruptive tram strike that led to shots being fired. After months of entreating the Consul, the sisters were allowed a brief visit to

---

15. From Eliza's Annual Letter, August 1927, 2.
16. Martha Clark, *Church Missionary Gleaner*, November 1927, 15.

Ningpo to see how the Girls School had fared. On arrival, as the front door was still sealed, they had to slip through a side door. They were shocked at a "picture of desolation. We peeped through the shutters but saw little furniture inside. The big school room which had been our joy and pride was empty except for one old desk: our drawing room and dining room had practically nothing in them."[17]

On their eventual return to Ningpo the sisters were frustrated that it took most of 1928 to restore the buildings and resume full classes in both the Girls and Womens Schools. Under the rule of the new government of Chiang Kai-Shek in Nanking, all foreign schools were now required to appoint only Chinese Principals. At St Catherine's, Eliza remained a senior teacher and worked productively with her replacement. Though there were continuing tensions about including Christianity in the curriculum, the school worked around the government regulations by holding scripture lessons before, and chapel services after, ordinary classes.

By the early 1930s civil war between the Nationalists and Communists was gathering momentum in some inland areas, and from 1933 Japan's occupation of Manchuria reignited long-held fears about its imperialist ambitions towards China. In Chekiang province, however, the political situation was relatively stable. Over the next few years their schools continued to grow and adapt to change. The number of pupils enrolled at St Catherine's doubled to 340 and a number of students won scholarships to undertake Higher Education in Shanghai. In 1935 compulsory co-education was introduced into all schools and Eliza, for the first time, taught boys as well as girls. Meanwhile, Martha was encouraged by rising numbers in her Women's School, which doubled in size to nearly seventy.

In mid-1937, however, Japanese forces aggressively crossed over the border from Manchuria, which in the following months escalated into full-scale war with China. In August the first decisive conflict was the Battle of Shanghai in adjacent Kiangsu Province. This began with air raids, followed by naval bombardment, military invasion and finally street-to-street fighting which lasted until November. Throughout these months, Japanese forces observed the neutrality of the International Settlement, but gradually won control of all Chinese sections in the city. The missionaries in Ningpo first heard about this fighting during their summer break and conference in the hills east of Hangchow. As Eliza writes:

> We very much realized we were in the middle of war, for not only were aeroplanes continually flying about but we could hear

---

17. Eliza Clark, Annual Letter, August 1928, 2.

the thuds in the distance and at night the order was to keep all windows darkened. On our return journey ... wounded men and military cars passed us and ... we reached Ningpo and found the city was very empty ... There is an airfield about five miles from the South Gate and the Japanese planes keep careful watch over it and bomb it at intervals ... on November 12, Sun Yet-Sen's birthday, five planes flew over the city, later they returned and dropped bombs. They missed the railway station, but the houses nearby suffered. Near the bus station there was more destruction. Our little English church St. Paul's, had many windows broken by the concussion ... It was decided to close the school but the sirens and planes passing made it difficult to hold classes and rumors were flying fast and furious.[18]

It was decided that all female foreigners should be immediately evacuated to the International Settlement in Shanghai. Eliza and Martha stayed in the China Inland Mission house. To cope with the flood of refugees escaping from the Japanese advance, one hundred and eighty makeshift camps had been set up. The sisters went to work at the largest of these at Chiah-tong University, just outside the French Concession. According to Eliza:

There were about 16,000 there during part of the winter. It was pitiful to see them. Their home was the piece of floor covered by their quilt. In some cases the neighboring families bedding was touching. The rooms varied in size. One large room had 167 people in it, another about 200. It was cold weather and the plea for warm clothes was insistent ... Some of us helped in the hospital, the sewing-room, where the tailors among the refugees were the workers. Others distributed clothes, others went from room to room to find the ones in greatest need. My sister was asked to oversee a house ... and I helped her downstairs, there were about 1000 people on the ground floors. Day by day, we tried to help these poor people, especially the sick ones.[19]

Martha adds: "Some of the scenes must remain in our minds as the acme of bitterness and distress ... Every day people died in the crowded rooms. The others who had come to the camp with nothing but a babe in their arms and children clinging to them, now saw their last treasures snatched from them by death ... As one of the missionaries said 'We felt that we had not been 'evacuated' but 'mobilised' by God in Shanghai to help in their time of extreme need.'"[20]

18. Eliza Clark, Annual Letter, July 1938, 1–2.
19. Eliza Clark, Annual Letter, July, 1983, 3.
20. Martha Clark, Prayer Cycle of the Chekiang Mission, January 1939, 3–4.

Refugees streaming into the International Settlement, Shanghai

Another eyewitness account by a fellow missionary from Ningpo reported that:

> The two Miss Clarks . . . have done splendid work in a large refugee camp here . . . The refugees were so grateful for their loving sympathy and help, that they collected a sum and presented with it a silver shield. It was a most touching thing. Some of the people of course are destitute and others have had little money, some earned a few cents a day . . . The response in the camps to the preaching of the Gospel is most encouraging. Chinese Christians go with foreign missionaries, and are doing a wonderful work. It is the same too in military hospitals. Chinese soldiers listen and gladly read Scripture portions, so that out of all the misery, opportunities are given for hundreds to hear and learn to read and Christians in many places are bearing witness.[21]

In the midst of this relief work, the sisters began to hear about horrific atrocities in Nanking, less than two hundred miles from Shanghai. Over several weeks Japanese soldiers carried out mass executions of men, women and children, as well as raping tens of thousands of women. The army looted and

---

21. E. Green, Letter to CMS Secretary, 20 April 1938, 1, 3. On Refugee work in the city more generally is documented in Ristaino, *Jacquinot Safe Zone*.

burned the city and established a puppet government in the nation's capital.[22] This so-called "Rape of Nanking" sent shudders through the whole population.

The two women arrived back in Ningpo in April 1938 emotionally exhausted but were grateful they could resume work in their respective schools. Encouraging news at this time was the reversal of Government policy prohibiting religious instruction to students. This was announced by none other than Madame Chiang Kai-shek in a widely publicized radio broadcast.[23] Disturbing news, however, was signs that the Japanese forces were now on the move towards Chekiang province. Hangchow was the first to be attacked and the sisters were concerned for their CMS and other colleagues when it fell to the Japanese.[24] Concerned for their safety, word came from CMS in London advising its missionaries to leave China as soon as possible. Even though Martha and Eliza were overdue for their next furlough, they believed God wanted them to remain and not forsake their Chinese friends and students.

經過死蔭的幽谷

The next year was full of uncertainty. Those at the CMS mission station knew that colleagues in Hangchow and elsewhere had prepared for Japanese invasion by filling sandbags and digging shelters to protect students and property against air raids. Stockpiling medical provisions for possible casualties, making an inventory of school equipment and library books in case they were destroyed also became a priority. While teaching continued in their schools, at most they could only plan ahead a term at a time. Because of troop movements in the province, their work in the countryside was severely curtailed. Despite this, a few other missionaries escaping from areas being overrun by the Japanese arrived in Ningpo. One of these was Mary Andrews, from CMS in Sydney, who went on to Lin Hai further south.

Eventually, on 16 July 1940: "Troops landed about twelve miles away and we had a refuge here and the people stayed for about a fortnight. We expected the city to be invaded but more Chinese soldiers poured in and the Japanese returned to their ships. So we settled down again. Owing to the blockade mails were most uncertain. Many Chinese and a few foreigners slipped in and out through the villages and islands along the coast. The journey was difficult and very dangerous. Junks were sunk but goods continued to come in. When

22. It is estimated that around three hundred thousand civilians were killed and somewhere between twenty thousand and eighty thousand women and girls raped.

23. This was reported in the *South China Post*, 9 April 1938.

24. The early days of this occupation are described in Bright and Ho, *War and Occupation*.

schools re-opened in late August: "at times planes were overhead and the gunboats were at the mouth of the river. However, on September 4th the city was bombed at about 9.30am and at 2pm; as it was bombed again on the 9th and 10th it was decided that the boarders should go to their own schools in the country. As the bombing continued on the 11th and 12th the teachers decided not to return to the city but I . . . carried on here."[25]

When the Japanese first invaded mainland China, they established a biological germ warfare unit in Harbin and for the previous seven years had been experimenting on local people with such pathogens as plague, anthrax and typhoid. Ningpo was chosen as one of the locations for testing aerial germ warfare. In late October 1940, planes dropped small odd shaped bombs containing fleas that carried bubonic plague on a part of the city. Within a few days people started to develop symptoms such as excessive vomiting, bleeding from the nose and mouth, and blackening of tissues in their arms and legs. To stop the plague spreading, city authorities acted quickly to isolate the most infected area and ultimately burn all the houses down. Since the students at St Catherine's had only returned the day after the bombs were dropped, on hearing about the plague the school was quickly closed again. This was just as well since, as Eliza wrote, "The plague was 100 percent fatal."[26] During November and December around 500 people died.[27]

Over the next four months, the city experienced a great deal of suffering, not only from effects of the plague but from continual air raids and shortage of food. As the Japanese soldiers advanced closer, between 80 and 90 percent of the population fled to the countryside. Finally, on 19 April, the Clark sisters received word that Japanese troops were entering the city. As the day progressed, the sounds of street fighting came nearer. They held their breath as they heard troops marching across the bridge towards their compound. As a niece of Eliza later recalled:

> A sizeable contingent of Japanese soldiers, bayonets at the ready, forced their way into the girl's school. She instructed all the girls to not be afraid, but to kneel in silent prayer, then, arms firmly crossed, placed herself between the soldiers and the girls and told their commander, 'You have come this far, but shall go no further.' There was what seemed a terrifyingly long pause, and they fully expected to be robbed, murdered, and worse, but amazingly, the commander grunted an order to his men who turned and left

25. Eliza Clark, Annual Letter, August 1941, 1–2.
26. Eliza Clark, Annual Letter, August 1941, 1.
27. See further https://contagions.wordpress.com/2012/07/14/japanese-use-of-plague-during-world-war-ii/.

without a word. "We must have been surrounded by prayer" was her explanation for their deliverance.[28]

Japanese soldiers occupying Ningpo

In the early days of occupation, the CMS missionaries had to register all Chinese workers on their campus, gain permission for trips across the bridge into the city, prepare for occasional tours of inspection, and guard the property against intrusion by drunken or looting soldiers. As foreigners had done in other occupied cities, those in Ningbo set up an International Committee to ensure their safety, protect their property and negotiate with the Japanese. The

28. From Hart, "Unshakeable Faith," 20–21.

foreign settlement area, including the CMS compound, became a haven for hundreds of Chinese. The Committee allocated money to the Mission to feed two hundred poor children in the city every day. "The hunger and want is very dreadful. What can be done? The children are just skin and bone."[29] The Mission was also asked to take in fifty children from the overcrowded orphanage, and to feed these Martha and Eliza had to beg, borrow and appropriate rice wherever they could.

This state of affairs continued until the Japanese bombing of Pearl Harbor on 7 December 1941 and following declaration of war on the Allies. All Western educational institutions in Ningpo were immediately shut down and every missionary placed under house arrest. With several others, the two sisters spent the next eighteen months confined to the Women's School. From this point on, their work was mostly restricted to individual contacts and pastoral activities. These involved personal counselling, organizing bible studies, and assisting in worship services. Their Chinese friends in the city visited when this was possible, but had to do this secretly to avoid the threat of punishment. Martha and Eliza found this experience of confinement a double-edged sword. On the one hand, the lack of "missionary" work to fill their days, and being limited to the same group of people day after day was challenging. The absence of information about the war from newspapers, the prohibition against owning a radio, and inability to receive any mail, was extremely trying. There was also the tension of regular inspections by their captors as well as not knowing what the future held for them. On the other hand, house arrest gave them more unstructured time for prayer, reading, writing a private journal, and just socializing with colleagues. It also gave them opportunity to invent creative ways of passing time, such as pursuing an interest and the occasional impromptu concerts. They also learned how to get by with few resources by improvising new ways of cooking, making clothes and repairing worn-out objects. Little did Eliza and Martha know that God would use this experience of house arrest to prepare them for what they would have to contend with during the next stage of the war.

During September 1942 all missionaries in the Chekiang were ordered to meet with Japanese authorities for interrogation. During these lengthy interviews they had to defend their presence in China, reveal their connections with foreign governments, and have all their details formally registered. These encounters were often intimidating and reinforced the missionaries' sense of isolation.

In June 1943, at the age of sixty-five, the twins were deported to a civilian internment camp in Shanghai. They were given just over a week to say their

---

29. St. Columb's Newsletter, November 1941, 2–3.

goodbyes and pack up their belongings. This meant drawing to a close almost four decades of their lives. Chinese Christians helped them buy and pack four small boxes of clothes, bedding, memorabilia, and a few books. "We've never had a such a week in our lives. We need not say much. Three visits from our Japanese 'friends' to say nothing of the others coming in all the time."[30] They were taken under guard to the docks and put on an overcrowded third-class steamer that took most of a day and night to reach Shanghai. They found this whole experience very trying. Despite this, a colleague observed, "for women of their age the twins were superhumanly wonderful."[31]

When they arrived in Shanghai, they were shocked to see how much of the city had been affected by air raids and street fighting since their last visit. From the docks they were bundled roughly into lorries and taken to what was formerly the Columbia Country Club in the International Settlement. The Club, once a place for Americans in Shanghai to relax and socialize, was an exclusive establishment closed to Chinese and Jews. Set on five acres of grounds in a fashionable district, it included a two-story house, built in the Spanish colonial revival style, tennis and squash courts, and an outdoor swimming pool. After the occupation, expatriates in Shanghai were confined there under a mild form of house arrest, but it had now become Western Area Internment Camp 3 for British expatriates from other provinces as well.[32] It was one of twenty camps scattered throughout Shanghai, which housed six thousand foreign nationals from ten different countries.

Martha and Eliza were lined up with their luggage and processed by their captors. All internees had to wear initialed armbands, "B" for British and "X" for all other nationalities. Since at the time Australians were still classified as British subjects, the sisters wore the letter "B" but were also given an identity number. As there were more than three hundred prisoners of war in the camp, every conceivable inch of space was used for sleeping purposes—hallways, verandas and bowling alley.

---

30. St. Columb's Newsletter, November 1945, 2.

31. *Open Door*, October 1943, 13.

32. The well-known author J. G. Ballard, whose book *Empire of the Sun* recounts the experiences of a young boy in a Shanghai internment camp, provides a brief description of the Columbia Community Club in his autobiographical book *Miracles of Life*.

Columbia Country Club, Shanghai

According to an account from an American internee in the camp:

> The Misses Clark have their sleeping, eating, and living quarters in a side gallery of a large open room, with 95 other men, women and children, the space for each individual being 7 sq. ft., pillars of the gallery and mosquito nets affording the only privacy. Each internee had taken his or her own bed and bedding, and the twins had warm bedding and clothing, and a supply of reading and writing materials. The camp had a library of 2000 volumes. Miss E.J. had all her labor in school work. Miss M.M. joined the vegetable squad, and rose regularly before 6am to wash the rice and prepare the vegetables for the cooks. Each internee taking a tray with a bowl for stew and rice and a cup for tea, with a knife, fork and spoon, filled their bowls from the line-up at the kitchen . . . Only five wash-bowls for 237 women and children and the sanitation problem seemed the greatest difficulty. Regular church services were permitted, Miss M. had been able to secure spectacles, and was radiant when once more able to read her Bible. The twins are frail (about 6–7 stone weight). As long as they can get enough extra food to supplement their diet I am sure they will have a fair chance of coming through. Their faith was indeed sufficient for them in all things.[33]

In such situations missionaries often played a significant role.

> Internment was in some ways easier for missionaries. They were used to moving, while for most of the others, it was the first time of not living in their own comfortable homes. In remote mission stations, missionaries often did not have entertainment at hand other than what they could make themselves. They were certainly

---

33. *Open Door*, October 1943, 12.

more likely to have experienced the relatively primitive conditions that most internees found themselves in. Though some were mistrustful and suspicious of the missionary groups in regards to their motives, they were a powerful force in the camp. They were also the trained educators, medical people, and efficient and qualified administrators. They had a common forum, were well organized, purposeful and could present a united front . . . Missionaries were often willing to tackle jobs which were unpopular. Many cleaned drains or latrines.[34]

The Japanese Commandant was a young, immature, ambitious man who frequently lost his temper. It did not take long to see that he was quite incapable of dealing with the camp's complex logistical and social problems. The sisters' long experience and understanding of Asian culture meant that they were often drawn into representing the internees in difficult situations. "Although scrupulously polite to the Japanese, they did stand up to the Commandant over issues of camp conditions. Their age, and the fact that their calming influence helped to run the camp smoothly, meant that they were often able to achieve success where others would have been reprimanded." When he was replaced: "his successor (found to be a Christian) on his arrival said 'I am glad to try to do what I can to help you. We will try to live together as a family.' The general morale of the camp was at once improved, and he did many acts of kindness."[35]

Daily life in the camp involved the constant stress of overcrowding, petty conflicts, lack of nutritious food and hardly any medical supplies. One of the biggest problems was poor sanitation. Although there were more than two hundred and fifty women and children, there were only eleven toilets for the whole camp. These conditions often led to dysentery, disease and death among older prisoners. On the other hand, there was room to walk around the spacious gardens, organize social and cultural activities, take part in regular church services and meet informally for singing and prayer. Every few months internees were allowed to write a postcard length letter home, restricted to a formulaic structure. The twins were able to get a few messages through to their family, church, and even CMS.

After nearly two exhausting years, on 28 April 1945, all the prisoners were moved to the Eastern Camp Centre at the Sacred Heart Convent Hospital in the Yangztepoo District. Internees were first marched under the watch of soldiers with guns and bayonets, then traveled in trams accompanied by

---

34. Leck, *Captives of Empire*, 321. On the wider issue of Australian non-combatants imprisoned by the Japanese see Twomey, *Australia's Forgotten Prisoners*.

35. *Open Door*, October 1943, 12.

guards on motorbikes and sidecars mounted with machine guns, and finally marched again into the grounds of the new camp. This consisted of ten two-story buildings with sagging walls and leaking roofs, surrounded by a twelve-foot high brick enclosure. Wiring and pipes had been disconnected, toilet and washing facilities removed, and drains were clogged. Crammed with around two thousand people, a third of whom were children, there was no space for common meals or recreational activities. Even beds had to be stacked on top of one another during the day to create room for people to move around. Food was frequently in short supply. On hearing about their near starvation diet, the christians in Ningpo found ways of getting food, and other necessities, to the sisters. This assistance continued till travel across the Yangtze delta to Shanghai became increasingly risky in the last months of their internment.

The camp was specifically established next to a Japanese army base and a large industrial area to deter American air attacks. When there were raids, bombs and shrapnel often came close. As the women wrote: "The Japanese were over the wall to the south and west of us, so if the expected invasion of Shanghai had taken place we would have been in for it."[36] When Japan finally surrendered to the Allies on 14 August, Martha and Eliza were very frail. The three hundred calories a day diet of the last few months had left them weighing only six stone each. As soon as their captors left, their friends from Ningpo began to visit, bringing "us chickens, eggs, cakes, fruit, soap, towels, notepaper, flowers, jam—everything they could think of."[37]

經過死蔭的幽谷

In the following weeks the twins underwent extensive health checks, interviews and arrangements for leaving the camp. As they had already missed one furlough, and were now past the normal retiring age, CMS assumed they would want to return to Australia. However, the sisters had no intention of doing so. They believed that God wanted them to complete the work begun in Chekiang more than forty years ago by re-establishing their schools. To honor their faithfulness, CMS reluctantly agreed.

On 20 October Martha and Eliza were the first missionaries to return to Ningpo, and were met by an enthusiastic band of Chinese christians. Along with their beds from the camp, they were carried in style by rickshaws through the streets of the city to the mission station. Church members had cleaned up their house and decorated it with flowers. The Red Cross had assisted by

---

36. Prayer Cycle of the Chekiang Diocese, November 1945, 7.
37. Prayer Cycle of the Chekiang Diocese, November 1945, 7.

providing meals. This rousing welcome was a great source of joy to them in the city they had loved so long.

During the weeks after their return, the women learned of hardship experienced by the local christians under the Japanese. Their food crops, animals and possessions were often commandeered, church buildings were demolished, and some believers suffered torture for standing firm in their faith. The sisters quickly set about refurbishing their schools, helped by the return of furniture hidden by locals during the Occupation. After Chinese New Year, the regular schools re-opened and most of the property taken over by the local government was returned. A greater number of students than ever before, more than seven hundred and fifty in all, enrolled with a devout christian Principal in charge. Other encouraging signs were ongoing house meetings and a mission led by young local evangelists.

The Clarks had planned to return to Australia at the beginning of 1947 but Martha became gravely ill. She spent two months at the American Baptist Hospital in Ningpo undergoing several serious operations. As she was not expected to survive, Eliza never left her side. The sisters had not realized how much nearly three years internment had taken out of them. Daily exposure to starvation, lack of sanitation, disease, and death as well as the experience of nervous exhaustion due to overcrowding, uncertainty about the future, and occasional air raids had all taken their toll. The after-effects of these were now exacting an additional cost. Fortunately, however, Martha's life was spared.

They left China for the last time in June 1947. Arriving back in Melbourne on 23 July, the twins were greeted by the Press as minor celebrities. Humbly they replied: "We saw all our work built up again and now we've come home to retire—that's the usual procedure!"[38] There were special welcomes at their home churches and at CMS headquarters. One of their first priorities was visiting the graves of family and friends who had died since they were last home sixteen years earlier. A highlight was meeting up again with the old "China girls" from Melbourne, including Victoria Mannett and Mary Armfield. After a year settling back in and fully regaining their strength, they engaged in extensive deputation work throughout the state. With the establishment of the People's Republic of China in 1949, the sisters felt the sadness and separation from their Chinese friends in Ningpo, and frustration at not being able to communicate lest they endanger them by association.

---

38. In *The Herald*, 26 July 1947, 5.

Martha and Eliza on deputation in Australia

For a while they lived with their sister-in-law, where they had often stayed on furlough.

> They lived in the attic room and were delighted that they could see the spires of no less than seven churches from their window. Their newly married nephew and niece, who also lived in the house, found it disconcerting when, unable to remember English words, they lapsed into Chinese dialect at the dinner table. The younger members of the family were fascinated by the fact that Martha always dressed in brown and Eliza in blue, and they found their stories of China and eccentricity enthralling.[39]

When, in the early 1950s, Dr. Max Warren, General Secretary of CMS in the UK, visited Australia, two of the people he most wanted to meet were "the famous Clark sisters."[40] Later in the decade Eliza and Martha moved south of Melbourne to the bayside township of Sorrento. They lived opposite the local primary school where, now in their eighties, every week they taught Scripture, and occasionally brought Chinese artifacts and dressed in Chinese clothes. In 1961 Eliza was diagnosed with cancer and admitted to the Royal Melbourne Hospital. Martha hardly leaving her side until Eliza's death later that year. On hearing about this, many of their former pupils, who had fled to Taiwan after the Communist Revolution, organized a memorial service in the

---

39. Hart, "Unshakeable Faith," 19–20.

40. On this trip, see further Max Warren, "Why I Came to Australia," *CMS Outlook*, May 1950, 4.

Protestant cathedral in Taipei. The legacy of the sisters' work continues today. In mainland China after the Revolution, Eliza's Girls School was fully merged with Trinity College by the Government, and eventually expanded to become what is now a leading High School in the city. Though Martha's Women's Bible School ceased after she left, an increasing number of women are trained full-time at the nearby theological seminary in Hangzhou and play an even more vital, upfront role in the province's thriving churches.

When asked whether she missed her sister, Martha replied, "Yes, but we did have 83 years together."[41] Though many assumed that Martha would die soon afterwards, this did not happen until four years later. At her funeral, the following words about the twins from the book of Revelation concluded the service: "These are they which came out of the great tribulation and have washed their robes and made them white in the blood of the Lamb. Therefore they are before the throne of God" (7:15, KJV).

---

41. From her obituary given in November 1965 by Rev K. J. Perry, General Secretary of CMS Victoria.

4

Rhoda Watkins

金指真

Hospital Matron—Kweilin

Rhoda Watkins

In the spring of 1924 ... the one-time ruler of the whole of Kwangsi appeared in Kweilin with his immediate band of followers ... shots were heard, and the fighting had reached the doors of the hospital.

Rhoda Watkins

The city gates were closed and never opened again for seventy-seven days . . . no communication at all was possible with the outside. Both sides had machine-guns and hundreds of rifles, and the attacking force possessed one big gun. Firing of rifles never ceased . . . and machine-guns . . . [raged] like a mighty thunderstorm . . .

After these battles, men were brought to the hospital with many desperate wounds, inflicted often by soft-nosed bullets, bringing back memories of the Great War . . . women entirely ignorant of the causes of the fight often received the most horrible injuries to head or trunk or limbs, injuries from which they could possibly never recover.

A missionary, one of two who had acted as mediators when the first robbers entered the city and who had received a gold medal for his services, was shot and killed instantly by a stray bullet . . . the chief Magistrate of the city, a fine old man with a notable family . . . was bound, taken into the street, and his head blown off, his body left lying in the street like a common criminal . . .

Starvation at last faced the city, all the rice in the granaries was exhausted. The poor could hardy obtain even a small portion of softly boiled rice. Gaunt forms stalked about the city, dogs disappeared, coffins were piled in corners . . . but as suddenly as the siege started, so suddenly did it lift."[1]

THIS DRAMATIC INCIDENT, ONLY a year into Rhoda Watkins's time in China, was in stark contrast to her upbringing on a peaceful family farm in rural South Australia. Born on 1 March 1894, she grew up with seven siblings on a small property in Lucindale, two hundred miles south-east of the capital, Adelaide. In her early years, life revolved around the farm, school and local Anglican church, with an occasional outing to the larger town of Narracoorte. When Rhoda left school at the age of fourteen, Rev J. T. Phair, the Rector and his wife employed her as a live-in nanny to their two daughters. The arrangement continued for six years until the Phairs moved to a larger church in Adelaide.

This coincided with the beginning of the Great War. Back home at Lucindale, Rhoda soon began to feel the impact of this conflict. Her two older brothers, along with a young man who she had intentions of marrying, enlisted in the Australian Army to support Britain in its fight against Germany. Their absence was followed by an unexpected personal challenge. Rhoda felt God spoke to her at church through a missionary on furlough from India.

---

1. Bacon, *East Meets West*, 63–66.

As he spoke of a life so different from that of a small Australian farm and told of the terrible disease and the superstitious fears that imprisoned the people among whom he worked . . . [she] knew with great certainty that this was how she wanted to spend her life. If she could help bring healing and the hope of the love of Christ to just a few of these people, it would be worth any sacrifice she might have to make.[2]

The following year, to prepare for missionary service, Rhoda began training at the Adelaide Hospital, where she lived in the nurses' quarters. Here she met Ethel Nunn, who had already begun training with the intention of offering for missionary service in Egypt. Over the next three years, Rhoda's missionary resolve was tested by touching letters from her young man in the trenches of France. Arriving home in Lucindale around the same time soldiers were repatriated, Rhoda knew she had to decide between marriage and children, or nursing as a single missionary. After considerable prayer, her conviction was that God wanted her to serve overseas. It was especially painful to break off the relationship with the person who had meant such a lot to her. Rhoda's family also found her decision difficult, preferring her to stay home and nurse George, the brother who had come back from the War with tuberculosis.

When, after a year, other arrangements were made for his care, Rhoda undertook a twelve-month midwifery course at the Women's Hospital in Melbourne as further preparation for working overseas. Finally, in 1921, she applied to CMS South Australia, only the second candidate after Ethel Nunn to be accepted. While training at St Hilda's in Melbourne, Rhoda also gained some valuable experience in parish work. Among both her fellow students and church members she was highly respected. Though softly spoken and naturally reserved, she could be both direct and decisive when necessary.

Holy Trinity Church in Adelaide, the oldest church in the city, offered to support her as their "adopted" missionary.[3] In mid-October, while Rhoda was at a Youth Rally, she received a cryptic telegram from CMS headquarters in London which read: "Watkins posted to Kweilin, China." Since she had no idea where Kweilin was, one of her friends at the rally climbed through an unlocked window of an office that was closed for the weekend, where there was a large wall map. He found out that Kweilin was in South China, inland from the coast, and a sizeable city. Not long after, Rhoda was advised by CMS about the luggage she should take.

---

2. Caterer, *Foreigner in Kweilin*, 1.

3. See the brief history of Holy Trinity Church 1936–2012 at https:www.trinitycity.church/about/history/story, 97–98.

"High on the list was 'one bath'. She compromised with a large galvanized iron tub and had a cover made with a lock. Inside she packed an enamel bowl and jug, a supply of saucepans and cutlery and crockery. It seemed as though she was going to the ends of the earth."[4]

經過死蔭的幽谷

Rhoda boarded a cargo ship bound for Japan on 8 February, 1922. This short, slight person who looked a lot younger than her years, was facing the adventure of her life. After three weeks in Hong Kong, her first exposure to Chinese culture, Rhoda received word that, because of a conflict between warlords in Kweilin, there was no possibility of going there immediately. Canton would now be her location for language study. She travelled in a train crowded with passengers, piles of belongings, soldiers and even a high-ranking General who, she heard the next morning, was assassinated as he stepped onto the platform. Rhoda then stayed at the CMS Boys School where language study occupied several hours a day. Her main challenge was learning the Mandarin form of Chinese spoken in Kweilin, while living in a Cantonese speaking province. "While I was in Canton," she wrote, "the bombardment took place by Sun Yet Sen so my stay there did not lack in excitement. Part of the time while the firing was on, we could hear the shells whistle over the Compound, but we were in no actual danger."[5]

In the summer Rhoda travelled to the mountain retreat of Kuling, on the lower Yangzte, where she first met missionaries from Kweilin. One of these was pioneer English doctor, Charlotte Bacon, who had founded the Way of Life hospital where Rhoda was to join the staff. In Kuling it was decided Rhoda should complete her language course—as well as study of Chinese classics, geography and history—in nearby Hankow.

Towards the end of the following year, word came that, though there was still some instability in the area, she could now proceed to Kweilin. Sailing down the broad and fast-flowing Yangzte was an unforgettable experience. After transferring to a houseboat on a tributary, the party passed through a brief exchange of rapid fire between opposing guerilla forces. This was a sobering reminder that China could be a violent place. The final part of the trip was by sedan chair. At the end of each day they slept in wooden beds covered with straw at simple inns.

---

4. Caterer, *Foreigner in Kweilin*, 3.
5. Annual Letter, 22 November 1922, 3.

Finally, the moment for which Rhoda had waited the past two years finally came. On reaching the Kweilin district she wrote: "The country is truly beautiful with all the ranges and hills in the distance. Every mile or two we passed through Chinese villages. Every village seems to swarm with children who crowd round your chair when the bearers put it down."[6]

When Kweilin itself finally came into sight, Rhoda felt it was like a dream come true. It was a traditional walled city whose scenery, according to a popular Chinese proverb, was "best among all under heaven." It was surrounded by "great, grey limestone rocks, which stand up like rows of jagged molar teeth from a flat plain. They even appear in the walls and centre of the city as great pillars of some mighty open-air cathedral of which the sky is the dome."[7] Kweilin was criss-crossed with canals connecting it to tributaries of the main river system that led to Shanghai. In 1923 it had changed very little from centuries before. Rhoda saw horses pulling carts in the streets, Confucian scholars wearing black skull caps and gowns, older women walking on tiny bound feet, beautiful wooden buildings with curved eaves and sloping roofs, half-moon foot bridges and perfectly manicured gardens. Western inventions, such as electricity and motorized transport had not yet penetrated the region. While there was a small wealthy class, the majority of people were poor, living in cramped conditions and food was frequently in short supply. Geographically, with its sub-tropical climate, and economically, through its trade links to Canton—the city belonged to southern China. Linguistically, through its use of Mandarin, and culturally, with its Imperial-like central square—it was more like northern China.

Within a short time, Rhoda replaced the current Matron of the Way of Life, who was starting a dispensary in Hunan province. Her responsibilities were supervising the nursing and administrative staff as well as the day-to-day running of the hospital. Along with Dr. Bacon, her first priority was developing a culture of care for the well-being of the whole person. This involved selection of staff who showed a genuine interest in patients, nurses who cared about more than medical needs, regular prayer for individuals by name and, where appropriate, sharing their faith. Rhoda regarded all this as being consistent with the name of the hospital.

---

6. Annual Letter, 22 November 1924, 1.
7. Bacon, *East Meets West*, 11.

View over picturesque Kweilin

Being a small institution, Rhoda had to be "hands on" in treating patients. As well as regularly with routine medical problems, at times, particularly in the humid summer months, the staff were called on to treat highly contagious diseases like cholera, typhoid, scarlet fever and tuberculosis.[8] In addition, she spent time visiting several small dispensaries in outlying towns and villages. Her experience of growing up in rural Australia was a real asset in dealing with cases where there was little access to medical resources. Rhoda assumed that this would be the pattern of work for the rest of her first term of service. However, wider social and political events regularly interrupted and brought unexpected challenges.

The first of these was the seventy-seven day siege described earlier. The second was the response in Kweilin to news of the shooting of students by British soldiers in Shanghai in June 1925. On hearing this, university students poured into the streets and gathered whatever weapons they could find. One shouted "Kill the foreign devil missionaries!" Several hundred young men set off for the home of CMS missionaries Rev Robert Bland and his wife. The students ordered them to come out and the two were pushed and jostled along the narrow streets to a chorus of abuse. After locking them in a disused office, the mob argued about what to do next. An angry student called out "There's

---

8. A good description of work in the hospital in this period can be found in the Kwangsi-Hunan Diocesan Newsletter, March 1925.

another one up at the hospital." Someone else yelled "But she's only a woman who hasn't been here long!" At the hospital "Rhoda had heard of the Blands's capture. The Chinese nurses had disappeared, frightened of the students, whose number had grown to several thousand. She locked the heavy front door and went to her room. There she knelt for a long time, praying for the safety of her friends and for sanity among the students. Then she lay on the bed, fully dressed, to wait for news."[9]

It was not until four hours later that Rhoda heard the Blands had been released and allowed to return home. Also, that a sedan chair with drawn curtains was waiting at the gate to take her to the American Mission across town. The next day, feeling against foreigners had subsided enough for Rhoda to return to the hospital but the local Bishop decided that she and the Blands should go to Hong Kong until the unrest died down. It took three months before things were quiet enough for them to return to Kweilin.

A third disturbance took place in March 1926 when a group of workmen and students sought to prevent pupils attending a christian Girls School in the city. One of the Chinese staff, Mr. Liu, tried to dissuade them but was seized by the crowd and dragged away. Hearing that the protesters were coming back the next day and concerned for the girls' safety, Rhoda and one of her medical team went to support the Principal.

> We found the gates guarded and soldiers placed there by the military officer in charge of the city. The soldiers let us through the gates, but no sooner were we inside than we heard drums banging and saw people running to take refuge in the school. We joined Miss Majors and the three of us with about fifty Chinese girls went to the top floor. The children were very much afraid as they had been threatened with all kinds of terrible things by the outside scholars. We could hear the noise of the crowd outside the gates and it did not sound at all pleasant. We had prayer with the girls and tried to comfort them. Suddenly we heard shots fired and we spent some anxious moments, wondering what had happened. A few moments later we had word to say that the crowd was dispersing and that the soldiers had only fired shots in the air to scare the crowd . . . we came back [to the hospital] as we heard that the procession was coming down this way. We were so relieved on arriving back at our own gate that all was peace and quietness.[10]

The following morning, the students returned in an orderly procession. They had branded the words "foreign slave" on Mr. Liu's face, and marched

9. Caterer, *Foreigner in Kweilin,* 31 and see also Bacon, *East Meets West,* 83–84.
10. Annual Letter, November 1926, 2–3.

him around the compound and through the streets of the city. Shortly afterwards he was ordered to leave Kweilin.

During this time, Rhoda was given the Chinese name Jin Set Sen, meaning "Gold pointing to the Truth." This helped her feel more at home and endeared her to the people, commenting: "I love the Chinese very much and thank God that He has called me to this service."[11] The Chinese themselves often proudly referred to her as "*our* foreigner in Kweilin."[12]

At the end of 1926 she took a well-earned furlough in South Australia. She visited her parents who had recently moved to another property in the Mallee district, and brought Chinese gifts back for relatives. Life in Kweilin had taken a lot out of her and she needed time to regain some equilibrium. One of the highlights of her stay was being the guest of honor at a reunion of nurses with whom she had trained at the Adelaide Hospital. During her furlough there were regular newspaper reports of continuing disturbances in China—increased fighting between warlords in some provinces, a major drought killing more than forty thousand people, and the outbreak of hostilities between the Nationalists and Communists. The prolonged evacuation of many missionaries from the inland provinces to the coast delayed her return by several months. So it was not until September 1928 that Rhoda arrived in Hong Kong and set out for Kweilin.

經過死蔭的幽谷

Having heard that the Way of Life had been looted by the Communists, and that the staff house had been burnt to the ground, she was naturally anxious to get back. Accompanying her was Blanche Tobin, a New Zealand missionary. They had been told by an American official that the safest route was by boat up the Pearl River through Wuchow. There they transferred to a smaller craft operated by a husband, wife and two young daughters. A short distance down-river, a Chinese militia officer informed them that, due to bandit activity ahead, the boat should take on a paid guard to protect them.

For a time everything was uneventful. Then, as Blanche was writing a letter and Rhoda, resting from sea-sickness, there was a sudden scream and sound of shots outside. Woken by the noise, the first thing Rhoda saw was the barrel of a gun pointed directly at her by a brigand through the window. Looking round she saw another man covering the tiny cabin with a second

---

11. Annual Letter, November 1926, 4.

12. This is recorded in the 200 Year Anniversary Australian CMS publication *Celebrate*, 64.

gun. Grabbing Rhoda's arm, and ripping off her watch, he demanded money. He took the small amount of money they both had and slashed open their cases with his dagger.

The two women heard the screaming of the owner's daughters as they were being dragged away from their parents. Fearing they were next to be kidnapped, Rhoda threw some clothes into a bundle and Blanche hid her bible and passport down her blouse. They were pulled off the boat and surrounded by other brigands, with guns at the ready. The two women and girls were forced to march so fast that Rhoda, still unwell, found it difficult to keep up. Frustrated, the leader of the brigands decided to leave her behind, ordering her to organize a ransom for the other three.

After returning to the boat, Rhoda sought out the nearest local official and, with his help, military assistance. She feared that the two girls, and even Blanche, might suffer violence or rape. The next few days seemed to merge into one as she threw herself back into work to keep busy. As weeks passed without an sighting of the brigands and their captives, her anxiety grew. The incident became a huge story in both the Chinese and overseas press. An offer by Bishop Holden to take the place of those kidnapped was refused. It was six weeks before Blanche, severely undernourished and frequently beaten, was released through payment of a thousand-pound ransom by a Chinese magistrate. One of the young girls was later released but the other was never heard of again. When Blanche finally stepped off the boat, her face and body were caked in mud, her feet were bleeding, and she could hardly stand up. Shocked by her appearance, Rhoda tearfully embraced her and the two thanked God for His protection.[13]

Over the next four years, Rhoda and her fellow missionaries experienced constant instability as a result of warlord rivalry and bandit activity. This frequently made travel to outlying dispensaries difficult. It also prevented a Chinese doctor getting through the war zone to replace Dr. Bacon who now had to return home to the UK for a time each year. One candidate was almost shot as a spy while attempting to cross the province and never made it to Kweilin. Though this situation led to Rhoda having to take on some of the doctor's work, she and Charlotte managed to start a new midwifery school for local nurses that attracted more than a dozen students.

---

13. Further accounts of Blanche Tobin's kidnapping appeared in New Zealand newspapers, such as the *Horohenua Chronicle*, 21 November 1928, 1–3.

Rhoda Watkins

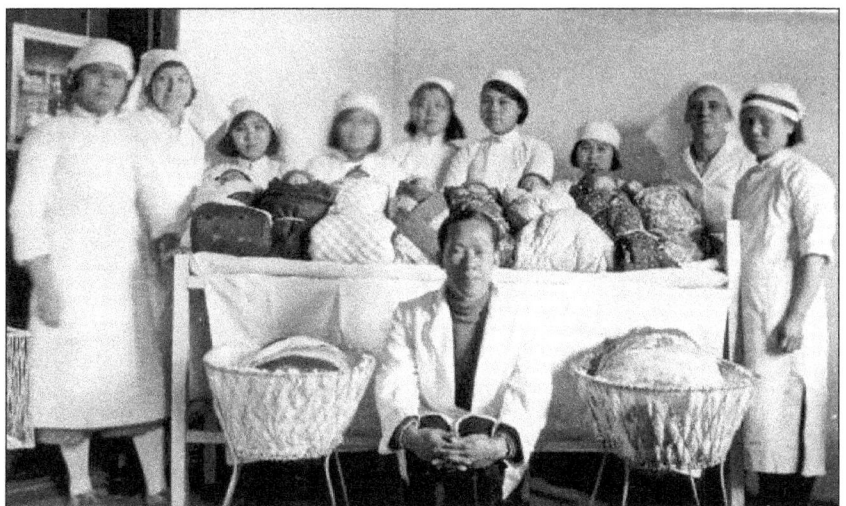

Rhoda and staff with newborn babies

In mid-1931 the city was caught up in two conflicts that affected the hospital. This was caused by the province asserting its independence from the central Government when Communist forces, under the guidance of the future Chinese leader Deng Xiao-ping, were also intruding into its territory. As Rhoda wrote:

> The Kwangsi armies made another attempt against the Government troops and suffered a severe defeat . . . The Government bombing planes were no mean factor in the cause of their defeat as the Kwangsi forces had no planes of any description to help them. July saw the defeated soldiers fleeing back . . . We attended a number of the wounded men in our hospital. Only those who were able to walk returned.
>
> In July the British Consul advised us leaving Kweilin if feasible . . . but on making enquiries we felt it would be safer in the city with the prospect of a siege than it would be travelling . . . We seemed to live in an armed camp at the hospital as our street was full of soldiers and the school at the back was full also . . . With the arrival of the attacking Government forces air raids began and we were made very uncomfortable from 7am until after midday. People made dugouts or else took refuge in . . . two caves in the bluff near the hospital to which we were able to go when we feared a raid . . . the daily gathering together for prayer during this time

was a constant help . . . many would come to join us when we met for public worship in the hospital hall."[14]

Fortunately, the siege only lasted a fortnight.

Main entrance to the Way of Life Hospital

Over the next eighteen months, work at the Way of Life continued to serve the medical needs of the people of Kweilin. A new venture was an evening program for teaching street kids to read as well as hear bible stories, to which some mothers with their babies also came. In the summer of 1932 Rhoda and her staff had to deal with the devastating effects of a cholera epidemic which caused much distress and many deaths in the city.

At the beginning of 1933, Blanche Tobin was bitten by a hospital dog. Rhoda suspected that the marks on her leg could be an indicator of rabies which was prevalent in China at that time. It was decided that this had to be

14. Annual Letter, 14 August 1931, 1–2.

checked out at a major hospital where she could get anti-rabies injections. The Bishop asked Rhoda to bring forward her furlough so she could accompany Blanche to Hankow where they had to wait for a month to ensure that the treatment had worked. It did, and in March the two of them sailed for home.

While she was back in South Australia, Rhoda kept in touch with what was happening in Kweilin. She found it incredible that her friends and family, still coping with the after effects of the Depression, should think that Japan's recent invasion of Manchuria, and ongoing civil war between the Nationalists and Communists, was so remote and unimportant. Since these events could prevent her going back to China at all, sometimes Rhoda felt quite isolated. In May 1934, shortly before word came about her return, she was invited to give an illustrated lecture in Narracoorte, and at a CMS dinner at Holy Trinity Adelaide.

On Rhoda's return to China in July, she was seconded for a time to a dispensary at Taochow which the Bishop wanted to become a hospital. This took place during the withdrawal of Communist troops from the area that was part of Mao Tse-tung's Long March to preserve and regroup his forces.[15] It wasn't until March 1936 that Rhoda finally resumed work in Kweilin.

After the fall of Shanghai the following year she wrote: "Now the war clouds gather over new China . . . and what the future holds it is hard to prophesy. Despite this one has to plan in faith that they will pass . . ."[16] A few months later, Rhoda describes the impact of further Japanese victories in eastern provinces. "Like most places in China these days Kweilin has been affected by the war though it is not in the war zone. With the great influx of refugees the life in the city seems altered and we notice the difference in our church life with the incoming of so many better educated Christians from so many more advanced cities nearer the east. One cannot help but see the Christians who have been scattered from their own centre taking part in our church life here."[17]

As these refugees flooded into Kweilin, the city began to look more like a smaller version of Shanghai, Nanking and Canton. Many of these had been leaders in their universities, professions and churches. Numerous war orphans also arrived from cities overrun by the Japanese and were cared for in one of the orphanages that Madam Chiang Kai-shek was establishing throughout Free China.

---

15. A concise account of the events leading up to and describing the Long March can be found in Hsu, *Modern China*, 57–63.

16. Annual Letter, 22 November 1937, 4.

17. Annual Letter, 12 September 1938, 1.

Shortly after the fall of Nanking and Canton, Kweilin experienced its first major air raid. This happened just after Christmas 1938. According to reports based on Rhoda's first-hand description:

> When Japanese raiders were sighted on the coast, maroon signals were given . . . If the bombers later turned inland heading for Kweilin, a second signal was given, and civilians and the military forces dived for air-raid shelters. At the hospital, an 8 ft. deep dug-out built in a zig-zag in the yard concealed 70 people. Nearby were three natural caves in the side of the mountain, which could accommodate 2000, 500, and 200 respectively. Chinese forces usually occupied the big cave, refusing to let civilians and other nurses from the hospital enter . . . The air-raids were worse than anything we had imagined. Huge fires were started by incendiary bombs and we saw whole blocks of wooden houses blown to pieces . . . We usually had 10 to 15 minutes' warning of an approaching raid—the shortest notice was 7 minutes for one raid . . . Bombs fell on other missions in other parts of the city, and 11 members of the staff of one were killed outright when a bomb fell upon a dug-out in which they had sought shelter . . . The northern end of the city, where Sister Watkins' hospital was situated had not been severely damaged as yet. The 40 patients were always dressed in the morning ready for instant evacuation.[18]

A few months later, all the American missionaries were ordered to evacuate Kweilin. The English CMS missionaries waited to hear their instructions from London. For months Rhoda had been feeling run down and was more prone to illness. It would seem that the cumulative stress of dealing with an overload of patients, many of whom were refugees, had taken its toll on her health. The growing frequency and unpredictability of air raids only exacerbated this. Though her furlough was due, lack of road transport and blockades of major rivers made it difficult to reach Hong Kong by boat. Word finally came through that Rhoda should take the first seat available in one of the few planes leaving for Hong Kong. She waited for days at the airport in Chungking before finding space on a mail plane that took off after dark just ten minutes before a squadron of Japanese planes bombed the aerodrome.

---

18. Recorded in the Sydney *Sun*, 2 June 1939, 7, and the Adelaide *News*, 13 July 1939, 10.

Rhoda Watkins

經過死蔭的幽谷

In July 1939, two months before the outbreak of World War 2, Rhoda was back in Adelaide. Shortly afterwards, under the headline "Women Also Serve," she was interviewed, with accompanying photograph, in the widely-read Australian Women's Weekly: "While several Australian nurses are undergoing their baptism of fire in France, Sister Rhoda Watkins, formerly of Adelaide is on furlough in her home State after experiencing shell fire in air raids in China."[19]

Between Christmas 1939 and Chinese New Year 1940, Kweilin was hit by further devastating air raids. In these, hundreds of houses were burned, the street containing the Anglican church was badly damaged, and more than "half the city was destroyed."[20] During that time Rhoda spoke at the CMS Summer School in Adelaide, passionately calling on Christians to pray and support China in its hour of need. After a clean bill of health, she was able to return to Kweilin towards the end of that year. On arrival, she found work at The Way of Life was in full swing. Dr. Bacon was also back but far from well. Because of the enormous influx of refugees, patient demands had increased and many had to be turned away. The Anglican church in the city also worked among refugees, and was grateful for the arrival and assistance of a new CMS missionary in the Diocese, Rev Eric Hague, with whom Charlotte and Rhoda soon formed a friendship.

With the entrance of the USA into the war after the bombing of Pearl Harbor, Kweilin became a base for the 14th US Air Force in China. A few months later, the city also became the temporary headquarters of the famous Flying Tigers, made up of three volunteer American squadrons who had already been fighting the Japanese for some time. Eric Hague volunteered to act as chaplain to a large, some of whom joined other internationals at informal gatherings in the hospital on Sunday afternoons. At one Christmas Day dinner, there was a French count involved in intelligence work, a British colonel heading up a military mission, an American university professor, and others from different countries passing through Kweilin. The city had become a kind of mini-United Nations.

During these years, Kweilin became one of the more progressive cities in China. In part, this was due to the enlightened rule of the warlord in Kwangsi. He liberalized its political life, initiated a variety of cultural activities and literary publications, encouraged the production of a range of newspapers, and sought to bring nationalists and communists into regular conversation.[21] The

---

19. *Australian Women's Weekly*, 4 November 1939, 45.
20. General Precis to the CMS Far East Committee, 7 March 1939, 21.
21. See further the thorough discussion in Zhu, *Wartime Culture*, 2015.

presence of well-educated refugees from eastern China and foreigners with international connections—as diverse as Ernest Hemingway and Ho Chi Minh—contributed to the development of intellectual groups and exchange programs. Those among them who were Christians also influenced life in many churches and schools.

Daily life, however, was now conducted to the sound and frequency of air raid sirens. "It was only possible to do marketing in the early morning, and the hospital relied on vegetables planted in every spare corner of the garden. Hospital clinics and church services were all dependent on the time of the raids. Each day a church service was held in one of the wards and most of the walking patients came, as well as the staff, even though sometimes they had to break off to make for the caves at a fresh alert."[22]

This chaotic routine largely set the pattern for the next three years. During that period, a small hospital radio was the main link with the outside world. In the first half of 1942 Rhoda was shocked to hear on the BBC that Japanese planes had bombed Darwin, Australia's northernmost city, and that enemy mini-submarines had sailed into Sydney Harbor and fired several shells. Though mail was intermittent, letters occasionally got through. This was how Rhoda received the unexpected news that both her sister Amelia and father had died during 1942. Though not knowing whether a letter would reach her mother at home, she had a strong sense that they were still linked by prayer.

Because the Japanese now controlled the major port and river system connected to Kweilin, prices became increasingly, sometimes weekly, inflated. In particular this made food very expensive and the only way the hospital could survive was via a Government concession that allowed them to buy rice at a fixed cost each month. During this time Kweilin doubled in size to almost half a million people and hospital staff increased to eighty to deal with the influx of refugees. This included two Cantonese doctors and although the hospital was built for only fifty patients it now accommodated many times that number. Patients come to the Way of Life because it had a stronger reputation for care than in the Government hospital. Alongside Chinese, these now included Indians, Portuguese, Russians, Eurasians, Americans and British. Consequently, Rhoda's workload as Matron became even more demanding and stressful. More than 1000 babies were born at the Way of Life during that year, many of them in the caves used as air-raid shelters.

In August 1943 Kweilin experienced its worst air raids so far. "There had been so many raids that people had become careless and didn't bother to go into the shelters but . . . instead of using big bombs that kill people outright the

---

22. Caterer, *Foreigner in Kweilin*, 104.

Japanese used little bombs that spread out when they hit the ground wounding people within yards. I have never seen such terrible wounds. The people were crawling into the hospital and just dying around us."[23] Shortage of food was also causing great concern. It made evacuation to the country districts for safety very difficult and was so dire that people sometimes resorted to cannibalism.

By Spring 1944, Japanese forces were closing in on Kweilin. Thousands more refugees crammed into the city and the days and nights merged in a nightmare of bombs, casualties, and lack of sleep. Every day the hospital grounds and verandas were full of people so they could be carried more quickly to the nearby caves for protection. Some evenings, to relieve the tension between air raids, Rhoda, Charlotte, and also Eric enjoyed moonlight conversations, sometimes in Chinese, outside the cave nearest the hospital.

Then, as Dr. Bacon reported: ". . . the blow fell. Like a tornado the Japanese swept down through the whole of our Diocese. Changsha fell . . . and 23 days later Sister Rhoda Watkins and myself were begged to leave by plane. All our other woman missionaries on Consular advice had already left . . . and so we left last with nine British Red Cross nurses . . . but with what heavy hearts. We had sung . . . and read together, with our Chinese staff, Psalm 121 that morning in The Way of Life Hospital."[24]

As the military defense was inadequate, guerrilla forces did their best to hold back the Japanese. Kweilin was one of the last cities in China to be occupied but before the enemy arrived, local forces enacted the official "scorched earth policy" and burned what was left of the city to the ground. "Two months later . . . total evacuation was ordered by the Chinese Government. What a scene, 350,000 people evacuating, walking, riding, on trucks, rickshaws, carts, by train, on the top of the carriages, in the carriages, on the buffers, on the steps, even under the carriages. Starving, ill of dysentery, cholera, caught by the enemy, robbed by their fellow countrymen, and scattered to the hills, and to near and distant towns and villages."[25]

---

23. Adelaide *News,* 28 October 1944, 3.
24. This appeared later in the Kwangsi–Hunan Diocesan Newsletter, May 1946, 13.
25. Annual Letter, May 1946, 13.

Kweilin devastated by air raids and fire

After leaving Kweilin in late June, Rhoda and Charlotte flew to Kunming in adjoining Yunnan province, which was still part of Free China. It was six weeks before Rhoda found a plane which took her to Calcutta, where she stayed until a berth on a ship going to Australia became available. Finally, a Dutch ship was found which stealthily sailed out of the harbor under blackout to avoid detection by enemy submarines.

Rhoda's initial reaction on returning to South Australia was culture shock. "When I first came back I noticed what lots of everything there seemed to be in the shops. It was strange to see plenty of soap which we never thought of buying in China because it was so dear."[26] After a few months rest she undertook some deputation, stressing the great need to rebuild the work in China as soon as the war was over. In January 1945 she gave one of the main addresses at the CMS Summer School and also spoke at Holy Trinity Church. Sadly, the gradual decline and death of her mother in February brought the whole family back to Narracoorte. Rhoda was grateful that she was home for this occasion, which for the first time enabled her to fully grieve the earlier loss of her father and sister as well.

In April, she was relieved to hear that the Japanese occupation of Kweilin had ended. This development enabled her to approach CMS about returning there. The dropping of hydrogen bombs on Hiroshima and Nagasaki in August signaled the beginning of the end for Japan. Rhoda was in Sydney in August 1945, seeking financial assistance for the hospital in Kweilin from a number of CMS supporting churches, when the allied victory over Japan was

---

26. Adelaide *Mail*, 15 September 1945, 7.

finally declared. Within weeks of the armistice in the Pacific being signed, she received approval from CMS to return to China. Reaching Hong Kong before Christmas, Rhoda was one of the first foreign civilians to enter the city. From there she eventually found her way to Kweilin via Wuchow on the Yangtze.

經過死蔭的幽谷

On her arrival in February 1946 she was joyfully greeted by her staff and Eric Hague.[27] They showed her what was left of the city, most of which now lay in ruins, including the Anglican church.[28] Though she had heard about the condition of the Way of Life, it was a shock to see that only the walls remained standing. It was also sad to realize that Dr. Bacon, its founder, was now unable to return.

Remains of the hospital on Rhoda's return

---

27. There are a number of graphic descriptions of life in Kweilin immediately after the war in Hague, *Close Encounters*, 208–20.

28. Interestingly, a piece of marble from this was sent to England and set into the new Coventry Cathedral. In return, a piece of the old Cathedral destroyed by German bombing during the war was sent to Kweilin and built into the new Anglican church there.

Awaiting her was a letter from Bishop Stevens explaining that, as there was no money to rebuild the hospital, not even from the United Nations Relief and Rehabilitation Administration (UNRRA) fund, he wanted her to go to Taochow Hospital instead. Hearing that the annual Anglican Synod was beginning in nearby Lin Lin, she traveled there with Eric the next day. At its meeting to decide future postings Rhoda, who rarely spoke out on such occasions, made a passionate case for rebuilding the hospital. After deliberation, the Synod granted her three months in Kweilin to see if she could raise the necessary funds. Even though this seemed a herculean task, she was convinced that, if it was God's will, a way would be found to do this.

Rhoda inspected the old site to see if there a place could be repaired to serve as living quarters. The best option was the central guest room which still had most of its walls. Sitting in that room on upturned boxes, she and Eric talked over ways and means of finding money. He offered to write to the UNRRA's Chinese branch (CNRRA) whose Director he knew. At an impressive afternoon tea arranged by Rhoda, the Director and some members of his committee offered to match every dollar she could raise. Thrilled, she wrote straight away to Charlotte Bacon in England and to CMS friends in Australia for financial help, pleading "If ever Kweilin needed our little hospital it is now."[29]

Money started trickling in from various sources—Dr Bacon and some of her contacts, a CMS clinic in a nearby town, the Shanghai Red Cross, a range of individual CMS supporters in Australia and Britain, as well as a significant gift from CMS Headquarters which the CNRRA quickly doubled. The provisional Government in Kwangsi made a substantial grant in recognition of the valuable work the hospital had done in the city. There were also some gifts in kind—from a Chinese builder offering to draw up plans, parcels from the International Red Cross with supplies of vitamin tablets and powdered milk—which were vital for near starving outpatients arriving daily at the hospital. These parcels also included many rolls of white cotton fabric which in the evenings Rhoda sewed into hospital linen and nurses's uniforms.

The strategy for rebuilding was partially shaped by the ongoing devaluation of the Chinese dollar as well as by the sporadic way donations arrived. As a temporary measure Rhoda used her dining room as a dispensary, with patients filing through much of the day. This gave little time for rest or privacy, and both staff and friends were concerned for her health. In March there was enough money to begin reconstruction and by August a thirty-bed hospital was up and running. A Thanksgiving Service was arranged to dedicate the building. For many people in Kweilin this was a symbol of new life returning

---

29. *CMS Outlook*, December 1946, 4.

to their city and hundreds came to share their stories of survival and hopes for the future. The chosen Scripture reading said it all: "Except the Lord build the house they labor in vain who build it" (Ps 127:1, KJV).

Thanksgiving for rebuilding

Due to the high stress of the last few months, Rhoda's health was now deteriorating. Regular bouts of high fever and gall stone pain often left her exhausted. Though the Way of Life was still waiting for a new Director, her load was partly alleviated by the appointment of a young Chinese doctor as well as three trained nurses. The second stage of rebuilding involved a proper dispensary, laboratory and a residence for the new nurses. As funds had now dried up, her own home still lacked glass in the windows and running water, and the hospital still needed vital equipment for inpatient care. Appealing again for money, Rhoda wrote: "It is a privilege to be back and though one is apt to get weighed down with difficulties over bad workmanship in building, inadequate staff and insufficient funds, still one feels God is with us and He is sufficient for all these things if we will have faith in Him."[30]

Around Christmas 1947, the much-needed replacement for Dr. Bacon finally arrived. Greta Thompson was a well-trained Cambridge graduate, whose parents had been CMS missionaries in China and in retirement were now helping to reconstruct medical work in another province. Like her predecessor, she had a particular interest in obstetrics and women's health. Rhoda

---

30. Annual Letter, 23 September 1946, 2.

was delighted by her appointment, describing this charming young woman as "our Christmas present."[31]

By mid-1948 the major part of the rebuilding was finished. There was an outpatient ward and waiting area, with rooms upstairs for each of the sisters, dormitories for student nurses and accommodation for a female Chinese doctor. Downstairs was the new dispensary, maternity clinic, laboratory, consulting rooms and X-ray facilities, though some equipment was still incomplete. Dr. Thompson and Rhoda shared a small residence together. Since her appointment as Medical Superintendent, Greta had quickly endeared herself to the staff and patients. She had also endeared herself to Eric Hague. Their wedding was held in Hong Kong so Greta's parents could attend and the young couple spent their honeymoon at the recently renovated St Stephen's College in Stanley.

During the rest of 1948 and first half of 1949, civil war intensified throughout the country and the Communists were increasingly gaining ground. In the neighboring province of Hunan they overran Taochow. Streams of refugees began to arrive in Kweilin as they had done during the war with Japan. In July storms and floods held up the Communist advance southwards but by September these entered the province and reached nearby Lin Lin. Rhoda was dismayed at the possibility of war now ravaging Kweilin again. She knew that in some parts of the country the Communists had been welcomed by the people but their largely anti-religious and anti-Western stance was troubling. "We don't go on the streets in the evening now and many people are leaving the city . . . None of our people [at the hospital] are leaving—there is nowhere to go and lots of others want to come in."[32] It was not long before the advancing army entered Kweilin. To her relief, this took place with scarcely a shot being fired.

There were several reasons why the Communists were unexpectedly victorious in China. After the war with Japan, the Nationalists did little to improve the dire economic and social conditions among peasants in rural areas. They also managed to alienate many in the cities, including industrialists, business people and students. Government propaganda failed to convince the bulk of people and corruption among their officials went on unabated. Chiang Kai-shek was at times a poor military strategist, and his armies lacked the conviction and cohesion of the revolutionary forces. By 1948 the Communists

---

31. Letter to Family from Rhoda Watkins, 8 January 1948, 1. A summary of her years at the Way of Life, entitled "My Time in Guilin," was shared by Greta Thompson for the 100th year anniversary, and may be found in, *Centenary Celebrations*, 17–28.

32. Letter to Canon Wittenbach, begun on 9 October and finished on 22 October 1949, 3.

were winning not just the military battle but the battle for people's hearts and minds.

In Kweilin, the presence of Communist forces in the city, and establishing of the People's Republic of China by Mao Tse-tung on 1 October 1949, did not particularly affect the missionaries or the work of the hospital. In the following months, however, a number of changes began to take hold in the city and province. Banners appeared in the streets announcing: "Labor made the world." Teachers were required to attend special courses for instruction in Communist ideology. Land was redistributed from families who had held it for centuries.

At the Way of Life, soldiers came searching for evidence of plotting against the Communists, leaving no cupboard unturned. For Rhoda, form-filling and record-keeping became an increasing burden. Permission had to be gained for travel anywhere outside the city or province. Nevertheless, the work of the hospital was not hindered in any way. Churches were also allowed to continue and services were well attended.

According to Rhoda, at that time:

> There was no open oppression of the church by the Chinese Communists, instead they resorted to a subtle ridicule of Christian beliefs . . . This is done very thoroughly. It starts in the schools with the very young. The Communists have been quick to seize on the Chinese horror of losing face. They will start by asking students 'Who believes in the superstitious belief that God created the world?' If a student says he does believe nothing is done to him. But his Communist teacher realizes how much face is lost every time such an answer is forced out.

In "self-criticism" meetings: "Small groups of men who work together, or who had something else in common, met about once a week and told each other what they had done during the week. They were frightened to do anything underhand in case their presence in a certain place and a certain time was questioned by some other member of the discussion group."[33]

By the middle of 1950, Rhoda realized that her days in Kweilin were numbered. American missionaries had already gone and, on the instructions of British CMS, the Hagues left shortly after the birth of their first child.[34] She was one of only two Western women now left in the city. Rhoda ensured that the Way of Life was placed under a board of management made up of hospital

---

33. Adelaide *Mail*, 17 February 1951, 10.

34. According to their son, who is a Professor of Medicine in Adelaide, the Hagues were "anticipating a return to China after the political situation had settled down." Personal letter from William Hague, 17 April 2019.

staff who each had a vested interest in continuing the various aspects of its work. The day finally came when a telegram from Australian CMS Australia arrived instructing her to return home. After a formal interview with the chief of police, it was a month before Rhoda received permission to leave. All she was allowed to pack for the journey was one trunk.

At her farewell from the hospital in August Rhoda was presented with a painting on silk in appreciation of twenty-eight years service. Her parting words to the staff were: "This same God of ours, who has brought us through many trials, is still with us. He will still love and care for you. Stand fast."[35] A sedan chair then took her to the railway station. Rhoda's final journey home had begun.

經過死蔭的幽谷

Returning to South Australia, she took a long time to recover from the strain and exhaustion of the past five years. Having spent over half her life in Kweilin, initially she found it hard to adapt to life in a changing Australia. She especially missed her Chinese colleagues and friends, and seemed to people at home in many respects to have become more "Chinese." By 1952, her health had improved enough for CMS to invite her as Principal of St Hilda's Women's Missionary College in Melbourne. Teaching and mentoring candidates heading to various parts of the world, she felt, was a great privilege. While there, Rhoda learned that CMS was seeking to relocate some of its ex-China missionaries to Malaya, where the Government had created new villages to protect locals from guerilla attacks by Chinese Communists. On hearing about the urgent need for experienced nurses in these settlements, in 1953 Rhoda offered to go. Initially she filled in at a number of village clinics, and then became Matron of a larger medical center clinic in Salak South, on the edge of the capital Kuala Lumpur. An Australian CMS missionary nurse, Kath Collett, joined her there, describing Rhoda as a "gentle person . . . [who] people in the Malay village loved."[36]

By 1958 Rhoda's eyesight worsened and she began to experience as series of severe heart pains. This led her regretfully to resign and return to Adelaide for medical treatment. The symptoms of Parkinson's Disease that had been developing over the last few years were now formally diagnosed. It was time to retire. In the early 1960s she was admitted to what is now the Julia Farr Centre in Adelaide, an institution for people with long term illness. There Rhoda

---

35. Caterer, *Foreigner in Kweilin*, 146.
36. From personal communication with Kath Collett, retired CMS missionary.

underwent experimental surgery to try and slow the degenerative process. Despite many frustrations, she came to view her illness as a test of faithfulness to God.

One of the greatest encouragements during this period was being made a Life Governor of CMS, the Society's highest international honor. Though she often wondered how the Way of Life would be affected by the new regime in China, little did she know that it was continuing to grow and thrive. It has remained the leading Maternity and Children's hospital in the city and, in 2010, commemorated its 100th anniversary. The main guest was Dr. Greta Hague, along with members of her family, who celebrated the event with current staff, former patients and their descendants, among whom were many christians. A television program about the hospital was aired on Chinese TV and its story was published in an illustrated volume. Rhoda was fondly remembered at this event, while at home she was honored among the pioneering women who have contributed to the development of Australia at the Women's Museum of Australia in Alice Springs.

Sister Watkins died in January 1975 aged 81 years. Her loving epitaph is best expressed by one of the people she served in Kweilin.[37]

Letter of Farewell

English translation

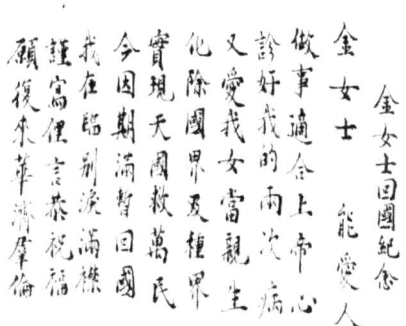

In commemoration of
Madam Jin's return to her homeland

Madam Jin - a loving lady
Her deeds in God's sight, so befitting
Her love for my daughter, so motherly
Twice, of my infirmities, she restored
Her deliverance knows no boundary-
Whatever nation, whatever race
What a witness to God's reign
As her term is fulfilled, parting is due.
My cloak is drenched as I weep o'er her adieu -
A rustic verse: my blessings for her
May she return to our mainland
And relieve many with her loving hands

By Jing-zhen Ye

---

37. Jing Zhen Ye, "Letter of Farewell," CMS Australia Archives.

5

Nora Dillon

梁民愛

Orphanage Superintendent—Limchow, Hong Kong, Shaohsing

Nora Dillon

Nora witnessed at first hand events that those who simply read about them back home found horrific.

"Japanese aeroplanes twice swept over Canton at 6.30 am today, reigning bombs on the town for two hours. Anti-aircraft guns and Chinese aeroplanes tackled the raiders. The Shameen Gate was closed to prevent Chinese stampeding into the European quarter. It is believed that considerable damage to property and loss of life occurred in the Chinese quarter . . . Tokyo newspapers describe their raid on Canton with 30 machines this morning and 15 in the afternoon as the fiercest in South China . . ."

"Canton, where Japanese bombers killed 3000 yesterday, is the largest, most turbulent and most politically-advanced city in South China. Because of the city's industrial importance, the blow dealt by Japan is severe . . . One of the principal targets of the Japanese bombers would be the Kwangtung arsenal."

"Whole streets of poorer dwellings in Canton are shattered to bits and limbs and mutilated bodies are piled high in utter confusion. In this shambles, hundreds of women, many insane with terror and horror, are searching for relatives. Others, not comprehending the reason for this slaughter from the skies, are roaming the streets with the pathetic bewilderment of children. Hundreds of frantic children are seeking their parents, crying pitilessly . . . There were heart rending scenes at the railway station during one of the raids yesterday. Foreign women, lying prone on the platform awaiting departure, saw hundreds of panic-stricken Chinese dive for shelter underneath standing trains, only to be killed when bomb explosions wrecked the carriages, it will be weeks before the city can be cleared of human remains. Foreigners, unable to face these ghastly witnesses of wholesale murder, express the greatest indignation, as the raid seemed to be directed against innocent noncombatants and not organized military objectives."[1]

Only a few years earlier Nora had not expected to end up in China at all. Coming from a pastor's family, missionaries from many different countries had passed through the Dillon's church and home. She had grown up with stories about wonderful women like Amy Carmichael rescuing children and founding an orphanage in India, and Florence Young working with the Kanakas in the Solomon Islands. Her father, Rev David Dillon, a well-known Anglican clergyman in Sydney, was impressed by hearing Robert Stewart in Sydney in 1892 and often told the story of the Saunders sisters to his children. Although Nora had heard of many Australian women going as missionaries to China from her teenage years, by 1927, when God spoke to her about serving him overseas, CMS was focusing on the new opportunities in Africa.

1. See respectively the Maitland *Daily Mercury*, 22 September 1937, Sydney *Daily Telegraph*, 25 September 1937, 3, and Perth *West Australian*, 24 September 1937, 10.

She was born Alice Nora Dillon in 1906, the youngest of five siblings. Although named after her mother, to avoid confusion everyone simply called her Nora. Growing up in Lithgow, in the Blue Mountains, and Gladesville, a middle-class suburb in Sydney, she was educated in both public and church schools. After the unexpected death of her father when she was sixteen, the family moved to the inner-city suburb of Ashfield, and soon afterwards Nora began working as a stenographer for a motorcycle company. Being something of a "tomboy," she enjoyed the occasional pillion ride with fellow workers and clients.

In the early 1920s, her older brother Fred began training for the ministry at Moore Theological College in Sydney. Nora found herself thinking about the possibility of training as well. In 1927 this was strengthened by a profound experience of what she called "full surrender" to God. The following year she began a two-year course of study at Melbourne Bible Institute (MBI), the leading inter-denominational missionary training center in the country. At the Commencement Service, Nora was challenged by the text Principal C. H. Nash chose for his opening address: "that I may know him, and the power of his resurrection, and the fellowship of his sufferings, being made conformable unto his death" (Phil 3:10, KJV). Knowing missionary service could involve hardship, possibly even death, Nora asked herself whether she was really prepared for the cost.

During her time in MBI's Women's Hostel, she made many lifelong friendships. With her closest friend, Hazel Thornton, Nora often enjoyed playing practical jokes. Together they did things like holding afternoon tea parties with scooped out pineapples secretly stuffed with newspaper as the main treat, and auctioning off their corsets at the college jumble sale. Reprimanded by the Matron both Nora and Hazel were told "you'll never make missionaries!"

After graduating, Nora returned to Sydney while waiting for CMS to make a decision about her placement. For some time she had considered going to Africa. But in early 1930 a British CMS missionary, Alice Bakewell, from Limchow in south China, visited Australia seeking immediate replacements for two women colleagues who had unexpectedly died. In her public talks, Alice mentioned the occurrence of bandit activity in her region. When asked by a reporter: "Did this deter people going to serve in China?" she replied "It did not!"[2] A nurse, Flora Broughton, had already offered to go, as did Nora soon after. In the time before her departure, she engaged in deputation and fareweled friends and family. On 23 September 1930 the two young women sailed for China.

---

2. Sydney *Daily Pictorial*, 7 August 1930, 8.

On reaching Hong Kong, they stayed for two weeks at the large St Stephens Girls School, which Nora thought "a magnificent place"[3] that was doing impressive christian work. As this was her first time outside Australia, the colors, noises, crowds, smells and language in this Chinese British colony were surprising and exciting. The next port of call was Canton, seventy miles up the Pearl River in nearby Guangdong Province. The travelers were invited by the Australian Principal of St Hilda's Girls School, CMS missionary Gertrude Bendelack, to stay for another two weeks. Over the next few days Nora began to see how much christian education could influence a large and diverse city. Little did she know that several years down the track, this tranquil setting would suffer destructive violence from Japanese air raids before her very eyes.

經過死蔭的幽谷

The women next sailed by steamer for three days south-west around the coast to adjoining Kwangsi Province. After arriving at the port of Pakhoi, where there was an established CMS hospital and leper colony, they travelled a further twenty miles by overcrowded bus to Limchow, an ancient walled city with around fifty thousand inhabitants. It had five massive gates, four being closed every night, with armed guards at the other. The CMS mission compound was just outside the walls. The climate was sub-tropical, and in summer the region was susceptible to typhoons. Not long after her arrival Nora wrote: "From my balcony, in all directions, I can see dozens of little bamboo-encircled villages. How we long at times to visit them all, carrying with us the Glad Tidings, but pressure of work and shortage of workers so far has kept us almost entirely at the very center of things."[4] In addition she had to learn the language, and get to know the city and its way of life.

While living outside the walls rarely made the missionaries nervous, occasionally they were shocked when the bloodied bodies of slain bandits were left near the City Gate as a warning to others. One of the worrying events of Nora's first year was the arrival of a Communist battalion reconnoitering the region. However, this so-called: "Western Army, which occupied the city for three weeks, left as quietly as it came in, without bloodshed or rapine, and many unbelievers came to the Christian service thanking God for their deliverance."[5]

---

3. Letter to Nash, 29 October 1930.
4. Annual Letter, 29 August 1931, 1.
5. See Wigram, *Weapons That Win*, 102.

It was not long before Nora began to settle into Limchow.[6] However, being gregarious, she found it hard being in a place that was off the beaten track. Apart from the four CMS missionaries, and a few German Lutherans, there were only a dozen other Westerners in the city. Sometimes she also found it difficult to be mostly in the company of older colleagues. The upside of this was that it enabled her to concentrate on language study. Nora found learning the local dialect, a form of Cantonese, easier than expected. This was partly due to her previous occupation as a stenographer, which had trained her to substitute symbols for words. Always willing to try anything new, she enjoyed using her faltering Chinese in a variety of everyday situations.

Once her first language exam was successfully over, Nora gradually established a working routine. Always wanting to identify with the local people, she dressed in Chinese clothes and styled her hair in an oriental bun. Two days each week were spent in Limchow visiting church members in their homes and workplaces, one evening training up a gospel choir, and on Sundays supervising the children's ministry. On Saturdays she took some women to a nearby village where they attracted crowds by singing and then sharing their faith with anyone who would listen. Twice a month she itinerated with a colleague or Chinese bible-woman to two larger villages, always taking advantage of local market days when hundreds of people were buying and selling. On such occasions Nora's gift for music was put to good use. After singing some gospel songs, there was always a brief talk and handing out christian literature. Every six months she made extended evangelistic visits to outlying villages where the mission was seeking to break new ground.

Nora's warm personality and obvious gifts were soon appreciated. At MBI her teachers noticed that: "She has a generous, spontaneous nature and a bright sunny temperament which will always make her a pleasant companion."[7] These qualities were a real asset when working with fellow missionaries and Chinese colleagues. Her keen "sense of humour"[8] often saved the day in awkward situations, and when she made cultural faux-pas. Nora's motto "to try anything once"[9] came in handy when faced with unfamiliar customs, like eating snake!

---

6. Letter to Nash, 4 January 1931. A brief account of previous CMS work in this region, as well as Hong Kong, may be found in Gray, Church Mission Society.
7. Report on Nora Dillon from Nash, MBI, 23 May 1928.
8. Letter to Tregaskis, MBI, 13 December 1931, 2.
9. Letter to Tregaskis, MBI, 24 April 1934, 3.

Chinese village children

Nora's first summer break with missionaries in the province took place on a "cool 2500 foot high mountain with 100 miles visibility on a clear day."[10] In the following years she mostly spent the summers in Hong Kong, staying in CMS boarding schools, and once traveled to southern India to visit a friend from MBI days who was working with Amy Carmichael at Dohnavur.[11] This gave her a good opportunity to observe at first hand this amazing orphanage.

Mostly throughout her first term in Limchow Nora encountered little external conflict. Occasionally bandits were a big problem. As she wrote during a summer break in 1933: "One night just before I came away these attacked a nearby village and after the screams and sounds of shooting it was a comfort to have such a great promise as "Fear not, for I am with thee" (alluding to Isa. 41:10, KJV).[12] Although military and political conflict was taking place in the north of the province, the following year she wrote: "politically and otherwise things have been wonderfully peaceful."[13]

Early in 1935 Nora received the first of several letters from her sister about their mother's declining health. Fearing the worst, she asked CMS whether her furlough, which was not due till later the following year, could be

---

10. Letter to Nash, 13 August, 1932.
11. See Elliot, *Chance to Die*.
12. Annual Letter, 31 August 1933, 2.
13. Annual Letter, 21 September 1934, 2.

brought forward. Arriving in Sydney in early August, she stayed sat the family home in Ashfield helping to care for her now invalid mother.

After an official welcome by CMS, Nora began deputation work in and around Sydney. The opportunity to spend some time with her brother, Fred Dillon, an Anglican minster in the Blue Mountains, provided a refreshing break away from family and speaking responsibilities. It was a particular honor when Nora was invited to give an address at the Croydon Bible College graduation in early 1936.[14] Present on the platform that day were Archbishop Howard Mowll and Principal Rev Benson Barnett, both of whom had served in China. Among the student body was a young woman, Mary Andrews, whose life was later to be associated with Nora's in a significant way. Mary recounts how Nora's testimony there, and later address at the Burwood Women's Intercessory Meeting:

> emphasized the great need for pastoral workers in South China. I returned to College after that meeting very burdened. It was my 21st Birthday and at the party that evening the conversation was about Miss Dillon's challenging message. The students said that during her address their thoughts turned to me as possible pastoral worker, I asked them to stop talking about the matter as my heart strings had been attacked all the afternoon. They said they would stop talking but continue praying. The next few days found me greatly exercised and praying much for guidance. I had always associated my call to service in China with the China Inland Mission. The Superintendent suggested I see the Church Missionary Society Secretary.[15]

Nora was greatly encouraged that her simple testimony could be used by God so powerfully, and this experience led to ongoing contact between the two women.

Within a few months Nora's mother finally passed away. The funeral brought her whole family together and was attended by a large number of people. After helping to settle her affairs, Nora took the opportunity to have some much-needed surgery before returning to China in late 1936.

On her arrival in Limchow, the Bishop talked with Nora about gaining broader experience in another province. He arranged for her to go to Canton. "In the middle of 1937 I was asked to spend some weeks in the district north of Canton with a view to opening up new work . . . However this was not to

---

14. From Nora Dillon's personal correspondence in Moore Theological College Library.

15. Excerpt from an unpublished autobiographical manuscript in the Mary Andrews Collection at Moore Theological College Library.

be, as the Japanese, who were out, so they said, to help their Chinese brothers, plunged that country into an undeclared war . . . which has brought untold suffering and misery to that peace-loving nation."[16]. In September "I again visited Canton and hoped to commence work in the city, but that too was frustrated, as air raids became an almost daily occurrence and the population of the city hastily evacuated to the more remote districts."[17]

Towards the end of 1937 it was decided that Nora should transfer to the staff of All Saints Chinese Church in Kowloon to work among the large influx of refugees who fled to Hong Kong from Canton just before it fell into Japanese hands.

> It was a pitiful sight to see the thousands of men, women and children, many of them in a state of exhaustion and many others wounded, come into our depots, some with a few possessions that they had been able to gather up, others with nothing at all except perhaps a child or two or a very old person in baskets slung across their shoulders, and all with the same grim tale of looting and murder . . . I was able to visit in hundreds of tenement homes and to hear of wonderful deliverances from many whose hearts had been prepared for the Gospel because of the experiences through which they had passed. Meetings for women in child welfare centers, individual and group contacts in the Street Sleepers' shelter, personal work in food distributing centres, were all splendid opportunities . . . I had the privilege of conducting a Service in Cantonese in the big prison for Chinese women and girls, and . . . have had the joy of seeing several of those women make open confession of their faith in the saving power of Jesus Christ and two of them baptized, one only a few days before she went out to pay the extreme penalty for murder.[18]

The following September, with fewer refugees coming into Hong Kong and work among them more organized, Nora was sent to St Stephens College at Stanley in the south of Hong Kong Island. Located in twenty-five acres of beautiful grounds on a peninsula overlooking the sea, this prestigious boarding school had facilities comparable to the best public schools in England. A previous Principal, Arthur Stewart, was the son of Robert and Louisa Stewart, and the current Head, Ernest Martin, was the husband of their daughter Kathleen. Nora's role was acting House Matron in the Preparatory School with:

---

16. Annual Letter, 21 September 1934, 2.
17. Dillon, *War-Torn China*, 2.
18. Dillon, *War-Torn China*, 2–3.

oversight of 20 small boys from some of the wealthiest Chinese homes in and around Hong Kong. The work was extremely difficult, as most of the boys came from homes where they were able to do exactly as they liked and who naturally resented the rather strict discipline imposed upon them at school. During that year I made fresh contacts through attending, and once a month conducting, a service for the fishing population of Stanley. Practically all the members of the congregation were 'boat' people, having been born on the water, and spending their lives there except for an occasional short visit to the village . . . It is encouraging to know that big work is going on—or was, up to the outbreak of war—entirely amongst the boat people in South China, with well-equipped Gospel launches.[19]

A year later, at the beginning of World War 2, Nora was appointed temporary Matron at Heep Yun Anglican School in Kowloon. Its name, meaning "united grace," was the consequence of a recent merger of two former CMS institutions, an orphanage and a smaller school. It now provided for over a hundred boarders and several hundred day girls. The next two years at Heep Yun were very busy, partly because she resumed some work among refugees and prisoners and partly because of the "on-call" nature of the work.

經過死蔭的幽谷

When, in September 1941, her time at Heep Yun came to an end, Bishop Hall appointed Nora as temporary Superintendent of the recently rebuilt Taipo Orphanage. Situated on top of a hillside, with stunning views out to sea, this was thirteen miles from Kowloon and just ten miles from the border with mainland China. It was an experimental co-educational boarding school for orphans, and those rescued from slavery and cruelty, the first in this part of the world. The girls were divided into families in separate cottages; the boys lived in a separate section. In age they ranged from just a few months to eighteen years. While the girls learned home-making and about how to shop and handle finances, the boys did outdoor work which included carpentry, farming and animal husbandry on several acres of virgin land. The stated purpose of the orphanage was "to train the hands and develop the minds of the children in order that they may return to the[ir] homes . . . with practical knowledge, by means of which they can bring new life and hope . . . to send out into the country districts of South China christian men and women who will be leaders in rural reconstruction."[20]

19. Dillon, *War-Torn China*, 3.
20. *Eastward Ho*, November 1937, 162.

Taipo Orphanage, Hong Kong

Originally Nora was intended to fill in for only six weeks, while the Superintendent went on her holiday, and then to go back to Australia on furlough. One of her co-workers was a New Zealander, Margaret Jennings. In the event of war with the Japanese reaching Hong Kong, Nora completed a hundred hours of hospital training to qualify for the Auxiliary Nursing Service. This agency was designed to free up trained nurses and hospital beds so they could deal with military casualties by sending civilian patients to a temporary hospital at St Stephens Girls School. Throughout her next five years at Taipo, Nora kept a diary summarizing each day's activities. Mostly this is full of domestic details about meetings of various kinds, difficulties in acquiring food etc., with only occasional references to larger incidents in the colony.

In late November, with large contingents of Japanese troops massing across the border, the military authorities in Hong Kong staged a series of simulated attacks on the British colony to prepare its citizens for the possibility of war. There were enforced blackouts, planes dropping smoke bombs and air-raid drills.[21] Having observed in Canton the devastating effects of Japanese aggression, Nora feared for the children in her charge. Finally, on 7 December,

---

21. For a first-hand account of events leading up to, during and after the Japanese occupation of Hong Kong see Drew, *Prisoner of the Japs*.

reality hit with two-fold force. At the very time news came of the attack on Pearl Harbor, a squadron of Japanese planes took off from Canton, and fifty thousand troops marched across the border into Hong Kong. Though British, Canadian and Indian forces, supported by local Volunteer Defense Forces, attempted to resist the rapidly advancing Japanese, they were heavily outnumbered.

It took only a few days for the invading forces to overwhelm the border defenses and advance down the main route towards Kowloon. As the noise of fighting neared Taipo, the children were sheltered in the safest parts of the building. Everyone was full of apprehension. Ahead of the soldiers, groups of looters ransacked shops, broke into homes, and stole people's possessions. It was especially nerve-racking when attacking and defending troops began firing at each other less than two hundred yards away. Soon a Japanese officer and guards entered the orphanage to commandeer one of the buildings for their headquarters. When Nora explained that "we were caring for orphans, they left us alone. We were frightened because of the number of young girls in our care but not once did the Japanese molest anyone at the orphanage."[22] Several days later the enemy crossed Victoria Harbor on to Hong Kong Island. It took only a week for them to conquer the whole island and on 25 December the Governor of Hong Kong finally surrendered. The day came to be known as "Black Christmas" and on Boxing Day the capitulation was formally signed.

Nora was appalled when she heard news about the horrific events that had taken place at her previous school in Stanley. Shortly before the British surrender, drunken Japanese soldiers entered the College, which was then serving as a hospital. Bursting into the wards, they brutally bayoneted wounded soldiers who were not able to hide and imprisoned the remainder and their nurses in two upstairs rooms. Later a second wave of Japanese troops arrived, who dragged off many of the nurses, serially raped and mutilated them. Nora was deeply upset when she learned that on Christmas morning her friends and fellow CMS missionaries Ernest and Kathleen Martin had been arrested. Tied up in a small room, throughout the day they were continually struck with rifle butts from head to foot. At nightfall, barely conscious, they were thrown into another small room with four British and eight Indian soldiers. For the next thirty-six hours they were left without food and water and only then released.[23] In the month following the occupation, an estimated ten thousand women and girls were raped and four thousand civilians killed.

22. Adelaide *Mail*, 18 January 1947, 10, speaking at Holy Trinity Church, Adelaide.

23. On this and other executions at Stanley see Emerson, *Internment Camp*, 2008, 56–79 and more generally on life in the camp. Ream, *Too Hot for Comfort*, 29–63 and Rowland, *Long Night's Journey*, 362–64.

Japanese soldiers crossing a bridge near Taipo

In early 1942 General Rensuke Isogai, head of the military government, announced that all captured soldiers and foreign nationals would be interned in prisoner of war camps around Hong Kong. Nora assumed that this included all missionaries and wondered what would be the fate of the children in the orphanage. It was a great relief, and an extraordinary answer to prayer, that: "Together with five other Britishers who were engaged in orphanage work, my fellow worker ... and I were allowed by the Japanese to remain at our post, to care for 100 or more girls and boys for whom we were responsible ... Enemy National Passes were issued to us by the Japanese Foreign Affairs Department which were to be shown on demand."[24]

Even though they were not interned in a camp, a small company of Japanese soldiers were housed in the grounds of the orphanage. This meant that the staff and students had to be very careful to show deference by bowing to, and avoiding eye contact with, the enemy. It was important that the older girls not talk to any of the soldiers lest this be misinterpreted. Only once did Nora feel personally threatened by a Japanese officer, when he gestured that her throat would be cut if she disobeyed in any way. While relationships with the Japanese at Taipo were mostly quite formal, Nora was grateful for the occasional exception. A Japanese interpreter, sent to make arrangements for an officer and his men to be billeted at the orphanage, turned out to be a

---

24. Dillon, *War-Torn China*, 5.

Christian. When, one day, he showed her his New Testament "we all sat for some time reading the Bible together."[25]

Apart from Nora's concern for her students's safety, the main challenge was finding enough food. Due to the Occupation, disruption of trade, expropriation of land and a large army to feed meant that food was increasingly in short supply. Rationing of necessities—such as rice, oil, flour, salt and sugar—was introduced. Only eight and a half ounces of rice per person per day could be purchased and, with growing inflation, fewer and fewer people had enough to eat. Many began to die from starvation.

Taipo Orphanage was helped by growing its own vegetables. Along with a very limited supply of rice provided by the Japanese, a philanthropist provided them with a few pigs to breed for sale. "We also reared rabbits, thus enabling the family to remember the taste of meat, about three rabbits making a meal for over 90 people and that about three times a year!" Purchasing additional food:

> had to be done on foot . . . this meant a four hour walk and at least one night in the city. As we had no lights at the orphanage our day began at day-light, and went on till dark; the children being sent to rest for a couple of hours at midday to try and bridge the gap that should have been lunch! It was pathetic to see them becoming thinner and less active. Food was the main topic of their conversation, and practically the only games the little ones played were those connected with buying and cooking make-believe food.[26]

In 1942 a few small anti-Japanese resistance forces formed in adjoining Guandong province. One of these, the Dong Jiang guerillas, collected weapons left by the British Army, and made occasional incursions into Kowloon to protect traders, kill Chinese collaborators and rescue some prisoners of war. One of their most daring exploits was the rescue of twenty American pilots who parachuted into Kowloon when they were shot down by the Japanese. Word also spread about the rescue of other airmen who had to ditch their planes in China after the famous "Dolittle Raid" by a squadron of B-25 bombers on Tokyo in April 1942 as a response to Pearl Harbor. Two of these landed close to occupied Japanese territory where Nora's friend Mary Andrews was working.

It was only after the War that Nora learned of Mary's involvement in the rescue of one of the aircrews who waded ashore from the wreckage of their plane near Lin Hai. Four of them were wounded, especially the pilot Ted Lawson. The fliers were found by sympathetic villagers who, helped by a band

---

25. Dillon, *War-Torn China*, 5.
26. Dillon, *War-Torn China*, 5–6.

of brigands, managed to evade a hundred strong Japanese search party. Over the next three days the airmen were brought by boat and stretcher to the city. Though not a nurse, the magistrate asked Mary to assist in caring for them at the former CMS hospital. A young Chinese doctor, also a Christian, two Chinese nurses and another missionary, treated their injuries. The second aircrew, including the squadron's only doctor, arrived the next day, all of them unhurt.

Lawson's injury, however, deteriorated, and the only way of saving his life was to amputate his leg below the knee. After prayer, the operation began, with Mary assisting and then watching him overnight. The following day Japanese reconnaissance planes looking for the airmen flew close by. The Americans stayed in Lai Hai for nearly a month before setting out on a lengthy trek to find an airfield from which they could fly back to the States. The first airfield uncaptured by the Japanese was in Kweilin, three provinces away. Mary later heard from Ted Lawson and the flight's doctor how much their crews had been impressed by the missionaries: "They were just plain, gentle, hardworking men and women more completely uninterested in their own welfare and comfort than anyone I'd known. Their days and most of their nights were devoted to us."[27] Mary also heard about the frenzied attack of Japanese soldiers in May on the local villagers who helped save the airmen. This resulted in the death of tens of thousands of innocent civilians in Chekiang and Kiangsu provinces in a tide of bloody revenge that lasted several months.

For the next three years, except on rare occasions when a passenger train was running, every week Nora or Margaret Jennings took it in turns to walk to the market in Taipo, and sometimes into Kowloon or even Hong Kong, to purchase food and other necessities. They were also sometimes able to attend a Chinese church service. At any point a soldier could order them to show their pass or risk being shot. Being one of the very few Westerners not interned, the women always wore their orphanage uniforms as an additional protection. Nora had heard that the Japanese secret police were routinely rounding up local people and executing them in King's Park, Kowloon, by beheading, shooting and using them for bayoneting practice. Wherever they went, homeless people were living on the streets. Many of the stores had been damaged, looted or closed. In both Kowloon and Hong Kong the streets were full of hawkers and sidewalk merchants selling imported products that been stolen at the start of the Occupation. At first the women were confused that English street names had all been replaced and it was strange to see Rising Sun flags on many of the stores. Though there was "the strange smell of decaying, rotten

---

27. Lamb, *Going It Alone*, 122.

food, human excrement, and unburied dead . . . you could find anything you wanted if you went far enough."[28]

Throughout 1943 and 1944,

> one of the most pathetic sights was the Chinese who passed along our road in the course of their business between Hong Kong and the outlying districts, in their efforts to procure rice, which was being sold at fabulous prices . . . We watched them grow weaker and weaker, some of them keeping on until they died by the roadside. Occasionally, in speaking to those who passed on the road we would suggest that peace and better times were not far off, and often the man or woman struggling under a burden would reply, "I will never live to see peace!" Another common sight, but one to which we never became accustomed, was of fleets of lorries laden with firewood, each dragged by ten to fifteen women, who were almost bent double as they strained, animal fashion, to move their loads up the long hills outside Kowloon. And this is in order to earn enough rice to avoid starvation for another day![29]

Amazingly, although in the orphanage food was short, not one child died from starvation. Each time there was a scarcity of food and clothing it was provided for in some unexpected way.

Throughout the Occupation, Nora received no mail from Australia. She did not know that, like Pearl Harbor, Darwin had also been bombed and that two Japanese midget submarines had shelled Sydney and Newcastle in the middle of 1942. Owing to the Japanese propaganda, she had no idea how the war was progressing. Sadly, it wasn't until her return home that she discovered her sister Winifred had passed away in May 1943. Towards the end of 1944 Nora wrote in her diary: "Oh Lord, how long? How my heart longs and prays for a cessation of all these wars and tumults. 'The whole creation groans in travail together—waiting for . . . and redemption of our bodies' (Romans 8:22–23)."[30] She didn't even know that her friend Kathleen Martin, partly as a result of deprivation at Stanley Prison Camp, only a short distance away, had died at the beginning of 1945.

In the orphanage,

> the days, months and years passed . . . ministering to the spiritual and bodily needs of the children, but in such a home the work could never become monotonous. Each morning we had prayers,

28. Drew, *Prisoner of the Japs*, 171, 209.

29. Dillon, *War-Torn China*, 5.

30. This prayer is the last entry in the diary she kept through these years, which is now in the possession of Elaine Dillon-Smith.

with a short reading and address after which the little ones had school for two hours, while the bigger ones dug, planted, or cut grass or wood. Knitting had become a real art for many of the girls . . . Never once even in the midst of hostilities, did we have to miss our Sunday service and after the first few months we also had Sunday School and evening hymn singing.

During their last Christmas together she added: "even though many of the material things were lacking, the true spirit was there, and even in the midst of war we could celebrate the coming of the Prince of Peace, and look forward to His coming reign, when swords shall be beaten into ploughshares."[31]

British Admiral, Nora, and students during Victory celebrations

In her diary for 1945 Nora records occasional and later continual air raids on Hong Kong by the Allies. During one of these the orphanage was struck but without anyone suffering injury or loss of life. Finally, on 15 August: " . . . after years of talking of 'T'ai Peng' (peace) and hearing rumors without number, you can imagine something of our feelings when the local Japanese-sponsored English news-sheet announced the surrender! . . . Any restriction at that time was more than compensated for when the [British] Commandos came to disarm and take over from the Japanese and during the two months

31. Dillon, *War-Torn China*, 6.

between the surrender and my leaving for home the Commandos treated us and the children royally."[32]

It was only then that the missionaries learned of the role bombs dropped on Hiroshima and Nagasaki had played in bringing the war to a close, though not before the Japanese, fearing their defeat, in some theatres of war had massacred prisoners, including women and children. When the Allied Navy arrived in Hong Kong, a highlight for Taipo Orphanage was the visit of the Commander-in-Chief of the British Pacific Fleet, Admiral Bruce Fraser, complete with photographs for the Press. The appearance of this article in Sydney's *Daily Telegraph* on 2 October was the first news the Dillon family had since 1942 that she was still alive.

經過死蔭的幽谷

Arriving back in Sydney in October 1945, thin and emotionally exhausted, Nora was pleased that CMS recommended complete rest for the first three months. Christmas was very different to the austere celebrations at the orphanage, though she missed the children and wondered what the new year would bring for them. In mid-January she spoke at the CMS Summer School in Tasmania on "The Hardships of the Women of China."[33] Shortly afterwards she took part in the 50th Jubilee Celebration of Deaconess House at which Mary Andrews was also a special guest. During the next six months Nora was asked to speak at a variety of events about life under the Japanese, one of which was broadcast particularly on a major radio station.

By the middle of 1947 Nora was longing to go back to China. Mary Andrews had just learned that CMS was sending her to Shaohsing in Chekiang Province. The work there had suffered severely throughout the war and local Christians asked for help in building it up again. Someone was needed to assist the Chinese minister and teach religious studies at the CMS school. Mary realized that a colleague was necessary to revive the work in the surrounding district and that Nora had the pastoral gifts to do this. The local CMS General Secretary liked the idea and sought approval from London.

Mary left Sydney in July, arriving in Shaohsing in September. Nora sailed three months later, via Singapore and Hong Kong. She was surprised that the latter had recovered so quickly after the war. After Mary met her in Hangchow: "The trip [to Shaohsing] took three and half hours by bus through farming country the latter being a network of canals over which the bus passes

---

32. Dillon, *War-Torn China*, 6.
33. Launceston *Examiner*, 27 February 1946, 4.

on stone hump bridges. This city, too, is one of canals, as is also the country in all directions, which give it the name the Venice of China . . . We even have a canal right at our front gate over which we cross on a stone bridge."[34]

Nora with Mary Andrews (on left) on their veranda in Shaohsing

Mary was delighted that the very person God had used to call her to China was now her colleague. In some respects the two balanced each other well—Mary was reserved, Nora was gregarious; Mary liked order, Nora was more spontaneous; Mary was mostly serious but Nora had a dry sense of humor. At times, however, Nora found Mary's extreme frugality and tendency to insist on doing things her way frustrating, especially since Mary was her junior and

---

34. Annual Letter, 6 January 1948, 1.

had less experience as a missionary. Overall, the Diocesan magazine summed up their joint contribution. "Shaohsing . . . is 'manned' by two lone women, Miss Andrews carrying a very full job in school and church in the city, and Miss Dillon . . . making valiant efforts to bring help to country parts of the four parishes in the Shaohsing area."[35]

During the next two years the women continued to strengthen the Christians, and devise new ways of reaching out to unbelievers. Occasionally they worked as a team, organizing bible schools for women that provided activities for their children. On the wider political front, conflict between the Communists and Nationalists was escalating and coming closer to their district. In one place shots were heard at night, followed by demonstrations and riots, creating a great deal of insecurity. Nora wrote around this time, "One wonders what will be the next major crisis."[36]

By late April 1949 the Communist forces, who had been gaining ground in the country through the previous years, were only a short distance away.[37]

> The city seemed to be in a fever which reached a peak on Saturday morning the 7th of May, with looting and lawlessness. People who had feared invasion now began to feel that it would not come quickly enough. Nothing could be worse than 'no man's land' for the government and most of the army had gone . . . [A] girl . . . came running along in almost a whisper 'They're in! Soldiers are on Pagoda Hill.' Soon people came saying they had seen the Army of Liberation and been told not to be afraid, not to close their doors, and to go on with their work. The whole atmosphere of the city changed, the fear abated and people breathed more easily. What a relief—a city occupied without a shot . . . [Nationalist] planes came on the following Monday, bombing and machine gunning the streets, which sent everyone into another feverish state, but it was not lasting. Since then days have been peaceful except when a number of soldiers came on to our compound, looking for somewhere to cook their rice, after which they slept on the CMS home's veranda before continuing their march: they were quite well behaved and polite. The street opposite . . . was alive with military for over a week.[38]

---

35. See the *Chekiang Newsletter*, February 1949, 3 and the comment by W. R. O. Taylor that "Miss Dillon . . . promises to be a great itinerator" in the issue 9 April 1948, 11.

36. Annual Letter, 20 July 1948, 1.

37. The most thorough account of the struggle between the Nationalists and Communists as it involved ordinary citizens is in Lary, *China's Civil War*. For a focus on the military and political course of events see Westad, *Decisive Encounters*.

38. *Going It Alone*, 180–81. The raids were described as mainly "nuisance bombing"

As all other Westerners had already been evacuated from Shaohsing, Nora and Mary wondered whether they would both be placed under house arrest. This situation of being occupied by the People's Liberation Army (PLA) reminded them of their earlier experiences during the Japanese invasion. Resonating with CMS UK General Secretary Max Warren's statement that missionaries in China were now "sailing uncharted seas," Nora felt that she could not remember "a year more fraught with change and uncertainty"[39] in all her twenty years in China, including Hong Kong.

On the positive side, the PLA made an immediate difference to Shaohsing. The city was tidier and more sanitary. Every spare piece of ground was put under cultivation. New crops were sown, such as cotton, and factories set up to process them. Industry was diversified so there was less dependence on wine which reduced heavy drinking in the region. The Army carried out operations to eliminate plague-spreading flies, mosquitos and rats. Prices were controlled, and foodstuffs were plentiful. While the women were apprehensive about how their work would be affected, "up to the present everything has gone on normally without interference and we have met with nothing but politeness from those in control."[40]

On the negative side, it became more difficult to obtain passes for travel. The authorities were concerned that meeting with other christians in small groups might lead to criticism or even action against the new regime. It often took months for approval to visit surrounding villages, or colleagues in another province. Heavy taxation, and the mandatory purchase of victory bonds, imposed by the new government on their church, almost forced its closure. High inflation reduced the value of overseas support for missionaries, and even though the two women lived frugally it became harder for them to stay. Nevertheless, the local christians pleaded with Nora "Don't go!" and one said "You eat such a little rice I should be able to make enough money to keep you and my son."[41] However the two women were shocked when their Chinese Bishop Kimber Den was suddenly imprisoned without trial. Nora was also tested on receiving news that her sister, Kathleen, had collapsed and died but still decided she should stay.

Conditions in Shaohsing worsened when:

> The Communists divided the city into regions for twice weekly 'eat bitterness' meetings at which people accused landlords, employers

by the Nationalists.

39. Annual Letter, 31 August 1949, 1.
40. Annual Letter, 31 August, 1–2.
41. Lamb, *Going It Alone*, 192.

and one another ... [and] attend meetings for political instruction, discussion and criticism. The "eat bitterness" meetings created suspicion, fear and disunity as the list of those accused of serious offences was nailed to light posts. Next day the accused were taken to open land, lined up beside a long deep ditch, shot and buried. The local Communist cadres introduced [these] meetings at church ... Everyone lived more carefully as each person was required to make public confession of faults, failings and mistakes in front of cadres. This was a reversal of Chinese tradition not to lose face ... Later, at the united service in the Baptist church, as soon as Mary finished her sermon, the cadre jumped up saying: "What she said is not true! Don't follow this foreign religion. They promise you good things when you die. We will give you good things now. We will teach the children there is no god. In ten years' time the churches will be empty.[42]

All churches now had to register with the Government and hand over their accounts to officials. They were given only a limited time to sever relations with foreign organizations. In an effort to stamp out belief in the Christian faith, clergy and religious teachers had to attend a three-month intensive course of Communist indoctrination.

Shaohsing congregation shortly before Nora returned home

42. Lamb, *Going It Alone*, 199–200.

As 1950 drew to a close, Nora and Mary felt that remaining in Shaohsing might create trouble for local believers. They decided that after sharing a last Christmas with them, it was time to leave. On 5 January 1951 they formally announced their resignation, bringing tears to the eyes of local believers. After applying for exit visas, there was a mandatory delay to see if anyone reported complaints against them. As none were made, the two women felt free to leave. In April there was a final moving service at which Nora and Mary were presented with beautifully embroidered handmade scrolls. A large congregation, ten times bigger than when they arrived, tearfully bade farewell and prayed for each other. After travelling by train to Hangchow, they went via Canton to Hong Kong. There they met with other departing missionaries from their province who gathered together to share each other's pain at having to leave their people and work. Nora was never to see China again.

經過死蔭的幽谷

Since Nora was one of the seven last Australian CMS missionaries to leave China, she was welcomed back with great interest. Deputations focused on what changes were taking place there, especially in the areas of personal and religious freedom. She was then invited by CMS NSW to join their home staff and placed in charge of women's groups, with the monthly Women's Missionary Fellowship being a key responsibility. Nora also continued to help in work among Chinese Christians in Sydney.

Often asked to speak at churches about what was happening in China, Nora usually began by saying that the new authorities were always polite and never accused her of being an imperialist. "There are two sides to Communism," she explained. No sacrifice is too great in its fight to turn a vision of a new world—without God—into reality. Its slogan is 'eat bitterness today, enjoy happiness tomorrow' . . . Its equality of the sexes was shown by the fact that a girl could rise to the same position in the Army as a boy."[43]

On the other hand, although the Communists introduced extensive land reform, this did not benefit the majority of people. Heavy taxes were also imposed on churches which they could not afford, forcing many of them to close down. However: "Don't think for a moment that now all Western Christians have been forced to leave China that the Chinese Church has finished. Quite the opposite. The fires of persecution have but welded the church into a solid body utterly convinced of its faith and completely dedicated to Jesus Christ."[44]

43. Hobart *Mercury*, 4 February 1953, 18.
44. *Boorowa News*, 1 October 1954, 4.

Nora enjoyed an occasional dinner in Chinatown with other returned China missionaries, such as Howard and Dorothy Mowll, Mary Andrews, Sophie Newton, as well as Victoria Mannett while she worked in Sydney. In 1958 she and her sister moved from the family home in inner Sydney to Wentworth Falls in the upper Blue Mountains. This brought them closer to their brother who was the minister of a neighboring parish. She felt at home there because the marked changes of seasons reminded her very much of China.

During the 1960s, Nora continued to serve CMS by acting as an examiner of prospective missionary candidates. Her personable manner, and wide knowledge of mission in Asia, prepared her for this important role. As two candidates at that time said:

> We remember her as that rare combination: warm, welcoming and understanding on the one hand; and very astute in her questioning of us on the other. She had no problem with my being a Methodist working in an Anglican church and school. She was more interested in whether we would be flexible and adaptable enough to work in a different culture and in a different churchmanship than we were used to. No doubt this came very much from her years under the Communists in Chekiang Province . . . She made an indelible impression on us.[45]

Two CMS missionaries in Kenya remembered Nora as a definite presence at CMS Headquarters, and also as a person of great good humor who laughed a lot and saw the funny side of things.[46]

The legacy of Nora's work in China lives on. When her colleague Mary Andrews visited the province in the 1980s, she found a vital church with over 600 members that remembered both with great fondness. Today it continues to minister in a province with one of the highest percentages of christians in China. When the orphanage in Taipo closed in the 1960s due to large-scale urban development, the proceeds from its sale helped expand its work exponentially under the name St Christopher's Home. This now provides residential care for children in small group homes and through foster care; a network of child-focussed services including pre-primary education and children's health development; support for recently arrived children from the Mainland who lack adequate family care. It is now the largest non-governmental welfare agency in Hong Kong.

---

45. Ken and Jan Goodlet, in a private communication.

46. In a communication from Rev David and Ann Hewetson. David was CMS General Secretary in New South Wales from 1971–1974.

Nora Dillon

Nora outlived her brother and sister by several years, passing away on 22 June 1974 at the age of 68. Jesus' words in Matthew 25 are a fitting tribute:

> Then the king will say to those on his right, "Come, you who are blessed by my Father; take your inheritance, the kingdom prepared for you since the creation of the world. For I was hungry and you gave me something to eat, I was thirsty and you gave me something to drink, I was a stranger and you invited me in, I needed clothes and you clothed me, I was sick and you looked after me, I was in prison and you same to visit me." The righteous will answer him, "Lord, when did we see you hungry and feed you, or thirsty and give you something to drink? When did we see you a stranger and invite you in, or needing clothes and clothe you? When did we see you sick or in prison and go to visit you?" The king will reply, "Truly I tell you, whatever you did for one of the least of these brothers and sisters of mine, you did for me." (vv. 34–40, NIV)

Epilogue

THE WOMEN YOU HAVE just met "through the valley of the shadow"[1] did not think of their stories as being anything exceptional. They thought of themselves as very ordinary people caught up in tumultuous events a long way from home. Working among women, children, students, the sick, refugees and orphans, all found themselves at times in life-threatening situations. Their experiences of conflict varied in kind and intensity, but each required enormous courage and creative responses. Believing they were in the place God wanted them to be, and confirmed by the warm response of the local Chinese people, helped them remain faithful.[2]

There was, however, a cost. For most, the ongoing effects of living through dangerous and unpredictable circumstances over many years, took its toll on their physical and emotional health. They were prone to insomnia, ongoing digestive problems, high blood pressure, neurological issues, and endemic fatigue. As well as these, psychological symptoms like disturbing memories, nightmares, and flashbacks, now associated with post-traumatic stress disorder (PTSD), tended to surface. Two of these women, of course, in the prime of their lives, paid the ultimate price.

This experience of suffering united missionaries with the Chinese people. Together they endured the onslaughts of armed conflict—subjugation, violence and terror—resulting in unimaginable wounds of war that lasted long beyond the horrific events themselves. This affected not only millions of its people—scarring individuals, fracturing families, dislocating communities—but also destabilized China as a nation. After eight years of exhausting warfare with the Japanese, and four further years of unrelenting Civil War, the whole country became confused and unsure about the values that once held it together. This led to a type of national trauma, resulting in long term grief

---

1. Psalm 23:4b (KJV).

2. For some briefer case studies of missionary work in life-threatening situations in other countries, see Eitel, *Context of Violence*, chs. 12–19.

and insecurity, leaving it open to any system that might provide some stability and way forward.

What helped these women cope in the midst of serious hostilities was a strong sense of trust in God, the support of missionary and Chinese colleagues, and belief in the value of their contribution to China and its people. Alongside the strength they gained from personal and communal prayer, Bible-reading, and strategies worked out in conversations, staff meetings and conferences, their sense of humor, directness, flexibility, and willingness to sometimes lose face, enabled them to forge a way through difficult circumstances. At times they misjudged situations and made mistakes, but sought to maintain a commitment to love and serve those around them.[3] Ultimately, however, because missionaries were forced to leave China and could go home, they did not experience the full aftermath of upheaval that faced the ordinary Chinese who had no way of escape.

According to a leading historian of China, the contribution of long-term missionaries was quite exceptional. These men and women had extraordinary opportunities to help the cities in which they lived. They offered sanctuary to local people in danger and provided essential medical care. In some areas, initially there was no relief work apart from the efforts of missionaries. Many of therm made heroic endeavours to save local people and were regarded as belonging to their communities. Their practical and sometimes sacrificial help led to many individuals and families being converted. As a result, while Chinese religions seemed to give little comfort during these times of armed conflict, the faith that actually flourished was Christianity."[4]

Sadly, the women in these pages did not live to hear about the full effects of their contribution. All of them had died by the 1980s when China began to open up again. The hope they clung to was that, despite the darkness of the moment, God would strengthen his people in China, and bring new life out of their suffering.

It seems fitting to close with the words of the great first-century missionary that many of our women's experiences paralleled:

> I have been constantly on the move. I have been in danger from rivers, in danger from bandits . . . in danger in the city, in danger in the country, in danger at sea . . . I have labored and toiled and often gone without sleep; I have known hunger and thirst and have often gone without food; I have been cold and naked . . . But [God]

---

3. In "Learning in Wartime," 47–63, C. S. Lewis makes the interesting observation that we do not learn something essentially different in such situations as learn more intensely and quickly.

4. These remarks are drawn from Lary, *Chinese People at War,* 30, 49–50, 138.

said to me, "My grace is sufficient for you, for my power is made perfect in weakness . . . that is why, for Christ's sake, I delight in weaknesses, in insults, in hardships, in persecutions, in difficulties. For when I am weak, then I am strong. (2 Corinthians 11:26–28; 12:9–10, NIV)

Bibliography

Andrews, Mary. Collection. Donald Robinson Library, Moore Theological College, Sydney.
Anglican Diocese of Melbourne Archives. Records on Mary Armfield, Eliza and Martha Clark, Victoria Mannett, Eleanor and Elizabeth Saunders.
Australian National Library Trove Website. Australian Newspapers and Magazines. https://www.trovecanberra.com.au/.
Ballard, J. G. *Empire of the Sun*. London: Gollancz, 1984.
———. *Miracles of Life: Shanghai to Shepperton*. San Francisco: HarperCollins, 2008.
Banks Linda, and Robert Banks. *They Shall See His Face: The Story of Amy Oxley Wilkinson and her Visionary Blind School in China*. Melbourne: Acorn, 2017.
Banks, Robert, and Linda Banks. *View from The Faraway Pagoda: A Pioneer Australian Missionary in China from the Boxer Rebellion to the Communist Uprising*. Melbourne: Acorn, 2013.
Banks, Robert. "The Influence of the Keswick Movement on Missionary Work in China 1880-1930." In *Lucas* Series 2, 9 (2015-2016) 49-72.
Barnes, Ian. H. *Behind the Great Wall: The Story of the C.E.Z.M.S Work and Workers in China*. London: Marshall, 1896.
Bays, Daniel. H. *A New History of Christianity in China*. Chichester, UK: Wiley-Blackwell, 2012.
Bays, Daniel and Widmer, E. *Cross-Cultural Connections and China's Christian Colleges 1860-1950*. Stanford: Stanford University Press, 2009.
Belgrave Heights Convention. Talk by Victoria Mannett. Melbourne. At http://bhc.org.au.
Berry, D. M. *The Sister Martyrs of Ku Cheng: Letters and Memoirs of Eleanor and Elizabeth Saunders*. London: Nisbet, 1895.
Boreham, F.W. "The C.M.S. in the Union University and Middle School, Chengtu". In *The Bulletin of the Diocese of Western China*. 118 (October 1933) 25-30.
Broomhall. A. J. *Hudson Taylor and China's Open Century*, 7 vols. London: Hodder & Stoughton, 1931.
———. *The Shaping of Modern China: Hudson Taylor's Life and Legacy*. 2 vols. Pasadena: William Carey Library, 2005.
Brotchie, Philip. "Importance of the contribution of Australians to the penetration of China by the China Inland Mission in the period 1888-1953, with particular reference to the work of Australian women missionaries". PhD diss., Deakin University, 1999.
Caterer, Helen. *Foreigner in Kweilin*, London: Epworth, 1966.

Bibliography

Chen, Joseph T. *The May Fourth Movement in Shanghai: The Making of a Social Movement in Modern China*. T'oung pao. Monographie 9. Leiden: Brill, 1971.

Chen, Zhongoing. *Modern China's Network Revolution: Chambers of Commerce and Sociopolitical Change in the Early Twentieth Century*. Redwood City, CA: Stanford University Press, 2011.

Church Missionary Society Archives. Annual Letters of Missionaries, The Chekiang Newsletter. Church Missionary Gleaner, Church Missionary Intelligencer, Church Missionary Outlook, CMS Home Gazette, Kwansgi-Hunan Diocese Newsletter, Personal Correspondence, Prayer Cycle for the Kwangsi-Hunan Diocese, The Open Door, West China Missionary News. At Adam Matthews Digital Publications. https://www.amdigital.co.uk/primary-sources/church-missionary-society-archive/.

Church Missionary Society Australia Archives. Letter to Rhoda Watkins. Records on Nora Dillon and Mary Andrews. Sydney.

Cole, E. K. *A History of the Church Missionary Society in Australia*. Melbourne: Church Missionary Historical Publications, 1971.

———. *Letters from China 1893–1895: The Story of the Sister Martyrs of Ku Cheng*. Melbourne: St Hilary's: Kew, 1988.

———. *Servants for Jesus' Sake: Long-serving Victorian CMS Missionaries*. Melbourne: Keith Cole, 1993.

Cunich, Peter. "Love and Revolution in South China: The Church Missionary Society and the 1911 Revolution". I" *Journal of the Royal Asiatic Hong Kong Branch*. 51 (2011) 143–69.

Dillon, Nora. *I Lived in War-Torn China*. Sydney: Church Missionary Society, n.d.

———. Papers. Donald Robinson Library, Moore Theological College, Sydney.

Dixon. Lesley. "The Australian Missionary Endeavour in China, 1888–1953." PhD diss., University of Melbourne, 1978.

Doyle, Wright G. *Builders of the Chinese Church: Pioneer Protestant Missionaries and Chinese Church Leaders*. Studies in Chinese Christianity. Eugene OR: Pickwick Publications, 2015.

Drew, Gwen. *Prisoner of the Japs*. New York: Knopf, 1943.

Durschmied, Eric. *The Military History of China*. London: Deutsch, 2018.

Eitel, Keith E., ed. *Missions in the Context of Violence*. Pasadena: William Carey Library, 2008.

Eliot, Elisabeth. *A Chance to Die: The Life and Legacy of Amy Carmichael*. New York: Revell, 2005

Emerson, Geoffrey C. *Hong Kong Internment Camp, 1942–1945: Life in the Internment Camp at Stanley*. Hong Kong: Hong Kong University Press, 2008.

Erth, Duke and Johnston, T. *Hallowed Halls: Protestant Colleges in Old China*. Hong Kong: Old China Hand Press, 1998.

Gray, G. F. S. *Anglicans in China: A History of the Zhonghua Shanggong Hui (Chung Hua Sheng Kung Huei)*. Episcopal China Mission History Project, 1998. At www.internationalbulletin.org/issues/1985-02/1985-02-071-gray.pdf/.

Hague, Eric. *Close Encounters of the Fourth Kind: From England to China Biographical Activities 1913-1959*. London: New Millenium, 1996.

Hart, Alison M. "An Unshakeable Faith: Two Missionaries in China 1904–1947." MTh diss., Leon Morris Library, Ridley College, Melbourne, 199? (exact date unknown).

Holy Trinity Church, Adelaide. History. Adelaide. At https:www.trinitycity.church.

Hsu, I. C. Y. *The Rise of Modern China*. 5th ed, New York: Oxford University Press, 1995.

Bibliography

Jowett, Philip S. *The Armies of Warlord China 1911-1928.* Atglen, PA: Schiffer, 2014.
Kerr, Gordon. *A Short History of China: From Ancient Dynasties to Economic Powerhouse.* Harpenden: Oldcastle, 2013.
Lamb, Margaret. Y. *Going It Alone: Mary Andrews—Missionary in China 1938-1951.* Sydney: Aquila, 1995.
Lary, Diana. *China's Civil War: A Social History 1945-1949.* Cambridge: Cambridge University Press, 2015.
———. *The Chinese People at War: Human Suffering and Social Transformation 1937-1945.* Cambridge: Cambridge University Press, 2010.
———. *China's Republic.* Cambridge: Cambridge University Press. 2007.
Lary, Diana, and Stephen MacKinnon, eds. *Scars of War: The Impact of Warfare on Modern China.* Vancouver: UBC Press, 2001.
Leck, Greg. *Captives of Empire: The Japanese Internments of Allied Civilians in China 1941-1945.* Philadelphia: Shandy, 2006.
Lewis, C. S. "Learning in Wartime". In *The Weight of Glory and Other Essays.* San Francisco: Harper, 2005, 47–63.
Loane, Marcus M. *Archbishop Mowll: The Biography of Howard West Kilvinton Mowll Archbishop of Sydney and Primate of Australia.* London: Hodder & Stoughton, 1960.
Lutz, Jessie G. *China and the Christian Colleges 1856-1960.* New York: Cornell University Press, 1971.
———. *Chinese Politics and Christian Missions: The Anti-Christian Movements of 1920-1928,* New York: Crossroads, 1988.
Mannett, Victoria. "Girl Students in Chengtu". In *The Bulletin of the Diocese of Western China.* 116 (April 1933) 8–10.
McMullen, R. J. *War and Occupation in China: Letters from an American Missionary in Hangzhou 1937-1938.* Edited by Charles Bright and Joseph W. Ho. Studies in Missionaries and Christianity in China. Bethlehem, PA: Lehigh University Press, 2017.
Melbourne Bible Institute. Report on and Letters of Nora Dillon. Melbourne
McCord, Edward. *The Power of the Gun: The Emergence of Modern Chinese Warlordism.* Berkeley: University of California Press, 1993.
Mowll, Howard K. Collection. State Library of Victoria, Melbourne.
———. "Twenty-four Days with the Brigands: Bishop Mowll's Personal Narrative" In *The North-China Herald and Supreme Court Consular Gazette.* (3 October 1925) 12.
———. "West China Seen Through the Eyes of a Westerner." Ninth Morrison Lecture. In *East Asian History* 34 (2007) 117–131.
Norris, Frank L. *Handbooks of English Church Expansion: China,* London: Mowbray, 1908. http://www.anglican.history.org/asia/china/flnorris1908/08.html/.
Ng, Peter T. M. "The Rise and Development of Christian Higher Education in China." In J. Carpenter et al. *Christian Higher Education: A Global Reconnaissance,* 68–89. Grand Rapids: Eerdmans, 2014.
Paine, S. C. M. *The Sino-Japanese War of 1894-1895: Perceptions, Power and Primacy.* Cambridge: Cambridge University Press, 2002.
Paterson, Cicely. *Celebrate! 200 Years of Taking the Gospel to the World.* Sydney: Church Missionary Society, 1998.
Stericker, John. *A Tear for the Dragon.* London: Barker, 1958.
Ream, Bill. *Too Hot for Comfort: War Years in China 1938-1950.* London: Epworth, 1988.

Bibliography

Ristaino, Marcia C. *Jacquinot Safe Zone: Wartime Refugees in Shanghai.* Palo Alto, CA: Stanford University Press, 2008.
Roland, Charles. G. *Long Night's Journey into Day: Prisoners of War in Hong Kong and Japan 1941–1945.* Waterloo, ON: Wilfred Laurier University Press, 2001.
Service, John B., ed. *Golden Inches: The China Memoir of Grace Service.* Berkeley: University of California Press, 1991.
Shan, Patrick F. "Triumph after Catastrophe: Church, State and Society in Post-Boxer China, 1900-1937". *Peace and Conflict Studies* 16/2 (2009) 13–50. https://nsuworks.nova.edu/pcs
Song C. T. "Letter of C. T. Song." *Bulletin of the Diocese of Western China* 51 (Nov. 1941) 8–12.
Stock, Eugene. *For Christ and Fukien: The Story of the Fukien Mission of the Church Missionary Society.* 4 vols. London: Church Missionary Society, 1904–16.
Taylor, Howard, and Mrs. Howard Taylor. *Hudson Taylor and the China Inland Mission.* 2 vols. London: Morgan & Scott, 1918.
Thompson, Greta. Centenary Celebrations of the "Way of Life" (Daosheng) Hospital in Kweilin, now Women and Children Hospital (1911–2011), 1 June, 2011, 17–28.
Walker, David. *Anxious Nation: Australia and the Rise of Asia, 1850–1939.* New Delhi: SSS, 2009.
Walmsley, L. C. *West China Union University.* New York: Church Board for Christian Higher Education in China, 1974.
Wasserman, Jeffrey. *Student Protests in Twentieth Century China: The View From Shanghai.* Stanford: Stanford University Press, 1927.
Watson, Mary E. *Robert and Louisa Stewart: In Life and Death.* London: Marshall, 1938.
Welch, Ian. H. *The Flower Mountain Murders: A Missionary Case Study Data Base.* Australian National University Research Publications, Canberra, 2011. At https://openresearch-repository.anu.edu.au/handle/1885/7273/.
———. "Missionaries, Murder and Diplomacy in late 19th Century China." Paper presented to the 2nd Australian National University Missionary History Conference, 27–29 August 2006. anglicanhistory.org/asia/china/welch_ANU2006.pdf/.
———. "Nellie, Topsy and Annie: Australian Anglican Martyrs Fujian Province, China, August 1895." Paper presented to the First Trans-Tasman Missionary Conference on Australian and New Zealand Missionaries at Home and Abroad, Australian National University, Canberra 8-10 October, 2004. At https://www.google.com.au/search
———. "'The Vegetarians': A Secret Society in Fujian Sheng province, China1895." Paper prepared for the Asian Studies Association of Australia, University of Wollongong, New South Wales, June 2, 2006, 26-29. At https://openresearch-repository.anu.edu.au/handle/ 1885/32004?mode=full/.
Westad, Odd A. *Decisive Encounters: The Chinese Civil War, 1946–1950.* Stanford: Stanford University Press, 2003.
Wigram, E. F. E. *Weapons That Win: The CMS Story of the Year 1931.* London: Church Missionary Society, 1931.
Zarrow, Peter. *War and Revolution in China 1895–1949.* London: Routledge, 2005.
Zhu, Pingchao. *Wartime Culture in Guilin, 1938–1944: A City at War.* Lanham, MD: Lexington, 2015.

www.ingramcontent.com/pod-product-compliance
Lightning Source LLC
Chambersburg PA
CBHW070918160426
43193CB00011B/1509